DOUGLAS SCOTT was born in Springburn, Glasgow and in 1976 he moved with his family to the Highlands to start their silversmithing business. Over the years he had interests in rock and ice climbing, diving and sea canoeing, but his love of archaeology and astronomy came together one day when his friend Ian Fraser took him to see the Bronze Age Edderton stone circle and its outlying standing stone, the Clach Biorach. Being shown these stones led Dougie to the most joyful and frustrating period of his life, as he began to survey and photograph the solar and lunar aligned prehistoric monuments all over Scotland for the next 40 years.

STUART MCHARDY is a writer, musician, folklorist, storyteller and poet, and has lectured on many aspects of Scottish history and culture both in Scotland and abroad. Combining the roles of scholar and performer gives McHardy an unusually clear insight into tradition. As happy singing old ballads as analysing ancient legends, he has held such posts as Director of the Scots Language Resource Centre and President of the Pictish Arts Society. McHardy is a prolific author and has had several books published, including *Tales of the Picts*, *Tales of Edinburgh Castle*, *The Quest for the Nine Maidens*, *On the Trail of Scotland's Myths and Legends* and *Edinburgh and Leith Pub Guide*. He lives in Edinburgh with his wife Sandra.

MOONRISE AT STENNESS STONE CIRCLE, ORKNEY

The Stones of the Ancestors
Unveiling the Mystery of Scotland's Ancient Monuments

DOUGLAS SCOTT and STUART McHARDY

Luath Press Limited
EDINBURGH
www.luath.co.uk

First published 2020
Hardback edition 2020
Reprinted 2022
Paperback edition 2024

ISBN: 978-1-912147-80-9

The authors' right to be identified as author of this book under the Copyright, Designs and Patents Act 1988 has been asserted.

The paper used in this book is recyclable. It is made from low chlorine pulps produced in a low energy, low emission manner from renewable forests.

Printed and bound by Robertson Printers, Forfar

Typeset in 10.5 point Sabon by Main Point Books, Edinburgh

© Douglas Scott and Stuart McHardy 2020, 2024

Contents

Map showing the locations of ancient monuments mentioned in this book	7
Note to the Reader	8
Acknowledgements	8
Preface	9
Glossary	10
Introduction	11
Timeline	15

PART 1

Interpretations by Douglas Scott and Stuart McHardy   15

The People of the Earth and Sky	17
Monuments, Measurement and Myth	20
The Monuments	23
Types of Monuments	26
The Builders	32
Alignments and the Power of the Sun	36
Myth and Remembrance	40
Rock Art	44
Touching the Ancestor Earth Gods	48

PART 2

Surveys by Douglas Scott   51

ORKNEY	53
Temples of the Sun and Moon	55
The Ness of Brodgar	66
The Ness of Brodgar Temples	67
The Ring of Brodgar	69
The Comet Stones	73
Maeshowe	77
LEWIS	85
The Great Stones of Calanais	87
NORTH-EAST SCOTLAND	89
Tom Nan Carragh, Strathspey	91
The Recumbent Stone Circles	95
Sunhoney Recumbent Stone Circle	95
Midmar Recumbent Stone Circle	98
Tomnaverie Stone Circle	100

PERTHSHIRE 102
Croft Moraig Stone Circle 104
Monzie Kerb Cairn 111
The Roman Stone 118
Cloanlawers 118
The Cleaven Dyke 126
The Orwell Standing Stones 128

ARGYLL 129
The Kintraw Cairn 130
Torbhlaren, Argyll 135
Cairnbaan Rock Art 140
The Temple Wood Stone Circles 143
The Nether Largie Stones 148

SOUTH-WEST SCOTLAND 155
Ballochmyle, Ayrshire 156
Cauldside Burn Linear Cemetery 161

Re-use of Monuments in the Pictish Period
by Douglas Scott and Stuart McHardy 167

Continuity of the Sun 168
Pictish Stones 168
Sun Discs 174
Edderton Stone Circle 178
Rayed Discs, Cup Marks and Pictish Symbols 180
Links to Christianity 180
Aberlemno, Angus 183

A Simple Guide to the Rising and Setting Sun and Moon 186

References 188

LOCATIONS OF THE ANCIENT MONUMENTS MENTIONED IN THIS BOOK

Note to the Reader

Part 1: Interpretations, written jointly by Stuart McHardy and Douglas Scott, provides an insight into the continuity of solar belief from the Neolithic to the Pictish period. The authors have their own particular areas of focus and individually developed methodologies. Together, they provide an overview of Scotland's ancient monuments.

Part 2: Surveys, presents 40 years of field work and research by Douglas (Dougie) Scott, whose archaeoastronomy notes complement his unique photographic record.

Both authors are mentioned in the text by their first names.

Acknowledgements

Stuart and Dougie would like to thank the following people for their help and encouragement in their research: Iain Fraser, Professor Thom and Archie Thom, Terry Kelly, Julian Clokie, Gill Hardan, Bob Gourlay, Alison Wilkie, Drew Turnbull, Sheila Fraser, Heather and David McAllister, Mhari and Norman Strachan, Graham Robins, Dick Raynor, Professor Martin Carver, Alistair Jupp, Maggie Struckmeier, David Connolly, Sian Mackenzie, Thomas Scott, John Wells, George Kozikowski, Ian MacHardy, Giles Carey, James Pieroni and Chris Menday, Colin Richards, Nick Card, Dr JC Orkney, Anna and Graham Ritchie, David Trevarthen, Dr Alison Sheridan, Dorothy Low and Arlette and Alain Cauderlier.

Preface

IN 1723, WHEN the Reverend William Stukeley watched the midsummer sunrise at Stonehenge, both archaeoastronomy and archaeology were born. But whilst archaeology forged ahead over the next 250 years, apart from a few champions during the 19th and 20th century, the very possibility of prehistoric astronomy was ignored. This was due to the prejudice that prehistoric people were savages who were incapable of astronomy. During the 1960s, Gerald Hawkins not only suggested that Stonehenge was aligned towards the midsummer sunrise but also to the maximum northern and southern moon over an 18.5-year period. Professor Alexander Thom came to similar conclusions from his surveys of monuments throughout Britain, but added that they were aligned to horizon notches to mark the lunar cycles to a high degree of accuracy every 18.61 years. Thom called these times the major and minor standstills. He proposed that the year had been divided into eight divisions each about 45 days apart. Thom further suggested that some monuments were geometrically shaped using Pythagorean triangles and a 'megalithic yard'; our ancestors were involved in scientific astronomy. Archaeologist Dr Euan MacKie – drawing from Thom's work and from the excavations of the large henges in southern England – suggested that from the cultural similarities found throughout ancient Britain the social power was in the hands of 'astronomer priests' (MacKie 1977).

Archaeoastronomer Clive Ruggles surveyed over 300 west coast Scottish sites to test Thom's high accuracy theories, and while he found nothing to support them, he did find general orientations towards both the moon and the winter solstice sun over at least one 20-year period (Ruggles, 1984, p.305–6). Dougie surveyed a large number of monuments throughout Scotland. They were also found to be generally aligned to the sun at the eight divisions of the year and to the moon near its major and minor standstills every 19–20 years. These included the monuments around the Ness of Brodgar temples on Orkney.

Drawing on decades of their individual research, Dougie and Stuart take the hard data of surveying and through a process of analysis that includes material from the oral traditions of Scotland's languages and the landscape itself, give a fresh take on how we can interpret our country's past. What has become clear is that certain ideas, beliefs and practices that the evidence suggests began more than five millennia ago, continued to have fundamental cultural importance for generations of the Scottish population well into historical times, and can be tapped into today, changing how we appreciate the past and what it can tell us. The Stones of the Ancestors are not so mute as once they were.

Glossary

SUMMER AND WINTER SOLSTIADS

These are the times when the sun appears to stop its north-south movement along the horizon. They occur around 21 June and December. The solstices are about 180 days apart, and the sun at these times will rise and set in the same positions for a few days.

SPRING AND AUTUMN EQUINOXES

The times of equal day and night and when the sun is halfway, or 90 days, between the Summer and Winter Solstices. These usually occur on 21 March and September. The Equinoxes occur some 90 days before and after the solstices, when the sun is at its halfway point at the equinoxes, with a declination of 0°. The sunrise/set in early November and February occur some 45 days before and after the winter solstice and they are commonly known as the Winter Quarter Times. The same can be said of the sunrise/set in early May and August, and are known as the Summer Quarter Times, which occur some 45 days before and after the summer solstice.

MAJOR STANDSTILL

This is the time when the moon every 19–20 years can reach its northern and southern rising and setting extremes each month for about a year. These lunar extremes lie beyond those of the sun at the summer and winter solstices.

MINOR STANDSTILL

This occurs about nine years after a major standstill, when the rising and setting northern and southern extremes for the moon are limited to within the winter and summer solstice positions.

AZIMUTH (AZI.)

A bearing in degrees, minutes and seconds clockwise around the 360° horizon from true north.

ALTITUDE (ALT.)

A bearing in degrees, minutes and seconds of the horizon.

LATITUDE (LAT.)

A line around the Earth's surface measured north or south of the equator in degrees, minutes and seconds. The equator has a 0° latitude. The northern and southern hemispheres are designated with + and - signs and the north and south poles therefore have latitudes of +90° and -90°.

LONGITUDE (LONG.)

A line which is measured from the 0° Greenwich Meridian through the north and south poles and around the equator in degrees, minutes and seconds. Any point on the Earth's surface can be found by knowing its latitude and longitude.

DECLINATION (DECL.)

This is the celestial latitude, which is also measured from the equator with a declination of 0°. Like latitude, the declinations of the northern and southern sky are prefixed with a plus + and - sign, so the points in the skies directly above the north and south poles therefore have declinations of +90° and -90°. Because the axis of the Earth is tilted at about 24° to its orbital plane around the sun, this causes the sun to rise and set along the horizon between midsummer and midwinter approximately every 181 days. Four thousand years ago, the sun at the summer and winter solstices had declinations of about +24° and -24°. By knowing the latitude, the bearing and the horizon altitude of an aligned monument, it is possible to work out its sky latitude or declination. These declinations were then converted to give the times and dates when the sun and major and minor standstill moon will rise and set in line with the monuments.

Introduction

SCATTERED THROUGHOUT WESTERN EUROPE are the enigmatic monumental remains of the Neolithic and Bronze Ages. The most famous of these is undoubtedly Stonehenge in the south of England; however, thousands of burial cairns, stone circles, standing stones and rock carvings are found throughout the British Isles and Europe. Watching the first gleam of sunlight pour over the Earth's rim to touch the stones is perhaps as close as we can come to the feelings and experiences of our ancestors of some 4,500 years ago.

People have been fascinated with the sky for thousands of years. We know from the Lascaux caves that over 20,000 years ago they painted the stars of Orion, while the star Aldebaran became the red eye of the fabulous Taurus the bull in the northern skies. These same constellations later formed the mythological beasts and gods in Egyptian, Greek, Roman and medieval zodiacs. Our ancestors would have perceived the raw power of nature as supernatural gods which they had to appease in order to survive. They would have reacted with the same awe to the dancing northern lights or the flashes of meteorites as they fell to Earth. In Part One we look at potential survivals of ancient beliefs and knowledge in the indigenous myths of northern Europe.

Dougie has been fascinated by the night sky since, as a small boy in a dark Glasgow street, he was scared almost witless on seeing the full moon rise for first time. This stimulated his passion for astronomy, and later for archaeology and Scottish-Irish folklore. During the 1970s, he began to look at the monuments of Argyll, while trying to understand Thom's ideas.

On learning of his interest in prehistoric monuments a friend of Dougie's, Iain Fraser, showed him the remains of the Bronze Age Edderton stone circle and its large outlying standing stone. This stone was also carved with the 3rd to 6th century AD Pictish symbols of a salmon leaping over a vertically placed solar/lunar Double-Disc and Z-rod symbol. Shortly after this, he contacted Professor Thom and was invited to his home, where he and his son Archie gave Dougie a theodolite to survey the Edderton stone circle. A survey shortly after this found that the standing stone marked the setting sun in early November and February, some 45 days before and after midwinter. Dougie immediately saw that these times were the same as the Gaelic festivals of Samhain and Imbolc. This took him back to the Halloween of his childhood, where the intense heat of the November bonfires caused the bright sparks to whirl up into the night sky lit by a cold full moon.

If the Edderton stone circle was over 4,000 years old, some kind of solar continuity seemed to have survived from the Bronze Age until the Pictish period. Dougie began to explore the idea by surveying hundreds of monuments throughout Scotland. This was done by taking timed theodolite sun sights of their alignments from the late 1970s to the present day. These surveys were calculated using the *Almanac for Land Surveyors*. Many of the archaeologists he met were dismissive of the ideas of archaeoastronomy, saying that they could not understand Thom's complex astronomical surveys and it was unlikely that such a primitive culture would have been capable of astronomy. Dougie therefore decided that the only way to confirm that the monuments were aligned to the sun and moon was to photograph these events. Over many years, hundreds of photographs of these mainly solar events were taken, of which only a few appear in this book. The gathering of this evidence was also part of experiencing something that hadn't been seen by anyone in thousands of years. With some monuments, this meant returning on many occasions, as often the sun would be hidden by cloud at the last moment. This sometimes took up to 30 years to achieve, but this was just part of the fun of confirming the solar/lunar orientations of these monuments.

Dougie was influenced by Thom's ideas and has great respect for him, but like Ruggles he did not find any evidence to support Thom's high accuracy theories. Dougie therefore resolved only to record what he found. Surveying and photographing these solar/lunar events from these monuments, along with their archaeology and their collective folklore, have given Dougie an insight into the beliefs of this time. Eventually Stuart and he met and shared their research, which was encouraged by archaeologists

Gill Harden and Bob Gourlay, Graham and Anna Ritchie and Alison Sheridan. Professor Richard Bradley got in touch with Dougie as he was particularly interested in his surveys of rock art and they met to discuss this in Inverness in 1992. Since then, Dougie has shared all his surveys and ideas about solar/lunar continuity with Professor Bradley. This was in hope that the fusing of these two disciplines could give a better understanding of the ritual use of these monuments. It was also hoped that this would help assuage the negative response to archaeoastronomy by some archaeologists. As many people find archaeoastronomy difficult to understand, this has been simplified to the times and dates when the sun or moon will rise in line with a monument; the survey information is also shown (azimuth altitude and declination), but this can be skipped by the general reader. This and the photographs can be used to guide anyone wishing to experience these events for themselves.

Since the early 1970s, Stuart had been researching the folklore of ancient monuments and their locations, and has lectured, broadcast and published extensively ever since on Scottish history and folklore. His involvement in Pictish studies – he was the co-founder of the Pictish Arts Society – led to a new understanding of the role of the Picts in traditional popular culture, which has changed his perception of our history and archaeology. This in turn led to an increasing focus on the Scottish landscape in his research over the past 20 years. From this he has developed a new approach to understanding Scotland's past called Geomythography, a topic on which he currently lectures at Edinburgh University's Centre of Open Learning. Over the years, he and Dougie have become increasingly aware that their fields of research were beginning to overlap and this in turn has led to greater collaboration.

Dougie does not believe in Earth energy, ley lines or spirits and has no religious beliefs. Stuart is slightly more agnostic. The ideas in this book are our own and are not necessarily held by any of the people mentioned above. Unless attributed to others, all the surveys and photographs in this book were carried out and are © Douglas Scott 2019.

Timeline

Until circa 14000 BC most of Scotland was covered in ice sheets. Some plants and animals did survive in 'refugia', areas between glaciers, but pre-12000 BC there is no evidence of any human occupation.

12000 BC	Flint artefacts found at Howburn Farm, Elsrickle, near Biggar.
11000–9640 BC	A mini Ice Age known as the Loch Lomond Stadial returned.
10000 BC	Stone implements found at Port Rubha an t-Seilich on Islay.
8500 BC	Stone tools found at probable temporary camp at Cramond on the Forth.
8240 BC	Evidence of Scotland's oldest house found at South Queensferry on the Forth.
7500–6500 BC	A range of shell middens identified in Inner Hebrides.
6000 BC	First known use of stone building in hearths on Jura.
3900 BC	Balbridie timber hall at Braeroddach Loch, Aberdeenshire. First evidence for pastoral agriculture.
3700 BC	Early farm site identified at Knap of Howar on Papa Westray, Orkney. Occupied for 900 years.
3600 BC	Cleaven Dyke, unique Scottish cursus structure built at Meikleour, Perthshire.
3500 BC	Cairnpapple ritual hilltop site in West Lothian. Used over a millennium and again in Bronze Age.
3500 BC	First use of Brodgar megalithic complex. Reused till at least 2000 BC.
3400 BC	Evidence of walled fields and stone houses at Scord of Brouster on mainland Shetland.
3200 BC	Scotland's oldest crannog in Loch Olabhat, North Uist.
3100 BC	Stones of Stenness raised on Orkney.
3100 BC	Skara Brae settlement on Orkney.
3000 BC	Pottery and stone quarry found on St Kilda islands.
3000–2500 BC	Westray Wifie figurine found.
2900 BC	Calanais stones raised.
2700 BC	Maeshowe on Orkney.
2700 BC	Probable origin point of recumbent stone circles of Aberdeenshire and Kerry in Ireland.
2500 BC	Ring of Brodgar Orkney.
2000 BC	Building of Clava Cairns, Inverness.
1500 BC	Creation of Bennachie hilltop site, used for over a millennium.
1500 BC	Traprain Law hilltop site in East Lothian – used till circa 150 AD.

1000 BC	Creation of massive Eildon Hill hilltop site near Melrose.
800 BC	Jarlshof settlement on Shetland, used till 8th century AD.
700 BC	The Ballachulish Goddess figure made near Glen Coe.
600 BC	Development of Atlantic roundhouses.
80 AD	First Roman incursion into Scotland.
120 AD	Raising of Hadrian's Wall from Solway to Tyne.
140–160 AD	Raising and manning of Antonine Wall.
140–160 AD	First reference to Picts, as Pexa, by Romans.
200 AD	Major incursion of Romans under Severus.
360 AD	'Barbarian Conspiracy', Hadrians' Wall overrun by northern tribes in conjunction with attacks on Romans on Continent.
410 AD	Departure of Romans from all of Britain.
4th century AD	Probable origin of Pictish Symbol Stones.

PART 1

Interpretations

Stuart McHardy and Douglas Scott

BALLYMEANOCH STONES, KILMARTIN, ARGYLL
NH 83368 96408 LAT. 56°06' 40" N LONG. 5° 29' 09" W

At Ballymeanoch in Argyll, when standing facing the cup marks on the western side of the smaller inner stone, the north-west stone, which is offset about half a metre to the west of the others, draws the eye to the left side of the dome-shaped hill where the northern midwinter major standstill full moon sets every 19–20 years.

THE CLAVA CAIRNS
NH 75762 44472 Lat. 57° 28' 24" N Long. 4° 04' 24" W

The midwinter sun setting in line with the passage of the NE Clava Cairn at about 3.00pm, 21 December 1989.

The People of the Earth and Sky

ABOUT 12,000 YEARS ago, the great age of ice that had held the Earth in its grip for 70,000 years came to a gradual end. Over the next few thousand years, our hunter-gatherer ancestors followed the herds north from Europe until they reached the area of the British Isles. Eventually, the melting ice raised the levels of the sea, cutting them off from Europe. Over ensuing millennia, they were joined by other immigrants and, about 6,000 years ago, Neolithic people began to settle and clear the forests for farming. Over time, they started to build large communal monuments such as the stone circles of Avebury, Calanais, Brodgar and Stenness.

The great burial tombs of Newgrange in Ireland and Maeshowe on Orkney, along with many others, were also built and used during this time for the collective burial of the dead. The surveys of these and the Orkney-Cromarty and Clava cairns have shown that their passages were deliberately aligned, so that the light of the sun at the eight divisions of the year, and the moon during its major and minor standstills, would have shone into their burial chambers. The solar and lunar orientations of the tombs – which are sometimes called 'spirit houses of the dead' – suggest that the sun and moon were venerated as powerful gods. Other people with the ability to smelt and cast bronze and gold arrived in Britain from Continental Europe around 4,500 years ago. These Bronze Age incomers started to build newer types of solar/lunar aligned monument, in which single burials were placed. Burnt bone and burials have also been found in association with standing stones and it is possible that they were a simpler type of burial monuments that were likewise aligned towards the sun and moon.

There are small hollows called cup marks, which are carved on thousands of monuments and rocks throughout Northern Europe. Sometimes these cup marks are surrounded by a number of rings, which can be pierced by a groove running out of the central cup mark. The function and meaning of these carvings are generally thought to be unknown. Surveys of cup marks on stone rows, the Clava cairns and the recumbent stone circles have shown that they were in line with the rising and setting sun or moon at regular times within the Bronze Age calendar. This also included spirals on monuments in Argyll and Galloway, which were likely derived from those on the midwinter aligned passage tomb of Newgrange in Ireland. Perhaps it was believed that each year, as the solar and lunar gods renewed nature, they also nourished the spirits of the dead. These may indeed have been sacred times, when the people asked their sky gods for good harvests and placated them with gifts and rituals through the agency of the ancestors, so that famine could be avoided. Similar Bronze Age solar beliefs can also be seen in the small bronze horse drawn chariot with a gold leaf sun disc from Trundholm in Denmark and the Nebra disc from Germany. Gold sun discs have also been found in other parts of Europe. There are also the Scandinavian and Egyptian rock carvings of solar boats, carrying the souls of the dead to the underworld. Solar and lunar chariots are also found in Greek and later Norse myths and such beliefs lasted until the medieval period as depicted in the 11th century AD Canterbury Cotton MS, Tiberius Astronomical Miscellany. The excavations of late Bronze Age sites on the higher ground show they were abandoned as they were slowly covered by a blanket of peat, due to the change to wet and cold weather.

The alignment of the passages of the Balnuaran Clava cairns to the midwinter sunset was first proposed by Boyle Somerville in 1923 and Dougie photographed this for the first time in 1989. Dougie's 1992 surveys also showed that the passages of the other Clava cairns were also aligned to the southern major standstill moon and to the sun in early November and February. Some of these cairns are graded in height to what look like false portals that are in line with the midwinter sun and with the major and minor standstill moon every 19–20 years (Scott, D. 2010, 2016). Surveys of the earlier Neolithic Orkney-Cromarty passage cairns and a number of the recumbent stone circles showed similar orientations. It was concluded that these different types of monuments had been influenced over time by those on Orkney (Scott, D. 2016). This strongly suggests that a solar continuity existed within prehistoric societies over thousands of years. The range of dates of the Clava cairns show that they were in periodic use from the early to late Bronze Age. A cremation dated to the Pictish period was also found near the central ring cairn (Bradley 2000: 117–19).

The sun and moon are also depicted on the 1st century coins of the Iceni tribe in Britain. Some of these coins depict the sun as a triple spiral, which was later used on Christian crosses in Ireland and in Scotland. The 19th century 'Celtic Art' expert Romilly Allen said of the triple spiral, 'these designs may well have had a symbolic origin as the triskel was a well-known sun symbol of the Bronze Age' (Allen 1904: 155). These symbols were also used on Pictish Double-Disc symbols. This solar continuity can also be seen in the times of the medieval fire festivals that were held at the eight divisions of the year throughout north-western Europe.

One of the standard processes of both history and archaeology is to consider the past in terms of perceived periods of time, in order to try to understand various types of evidence, that evidence being contrasted and compared with other similar contemporaneous material. While this approach is of considerable value to the specialist, it is not the only way of approaching the past. In the process of investigating the Aberlemno roadside Pictish symbol stones, Dougie's surveys and photographs showed that they were aligned on the midwinter sunset and on the northern moonrise. The Serpent Stone is carved with a snake, a mirror and comb, a large solar/lunar Double-Disc and Z-rod. There are six cup marks on its other side. The Crescent Stone stands a short distance to the south-west and is carved with a slim crescent. Professor Charles Thomas dated the early Pictish symbols to the 3rd century AD (Thomas c.1963). This suggests that these and other Pictish symbols were carved on Bronze Age standing stones.

It is generally accepted that the early Pictish symbols date from the 1st millennium AD. The people who carved these symbols may have been re-using stones set in place by their ancestors in the period from the Bronze Age to the 1st millennium AD; or, they may have been following inherited patterns of behaviour, as shown in Stuart's research, in which he draws attention to pre-Christian ideas behind the earliest Pictish symbols, that likewise appear to be of considerable antiquity (McHardy 2012 *passim*). Much of this analysis is drawn from what was originally oral tradition and is generally referred to as folklore, material handed down locally over generations without the use of literature in any form. Dougie has also drawn attention to the potential value of such folklore in helping us better understand ancient monuments and recently Stuart has been working on an interdisciplinary process between archaeology and folklore, analysing specific sites which appear to have held considerable significance for local communities over long periods of time. The use of alignments on which much of this book focuses is clear evidence of the understanding ancient peoples had of the importance of the sun and moon. This understanding of and apparent reverence for these celestial bodies must have long predated the arrival of people in what we now know as Scotland and the rest of post-Ice Age northern Europe.

In synthesising or closely linking the forms of analysis developed by the authors, this work approaches the symbol stones of the Picts not as an isolated and stratified series of typological constructs but as evidence of cultural continuity and it provides a series of specific examples that support the idea of such cultural continuity in Scotland's past – a continuity that is reinforced by the pattern of occupation of most of Scotland's habitable areas over several millennia. Consisting of small-scale, self-sufficient pastoral communities scattered across the landscape, referred to as fermtouns in Lowland and clachans in Highland areas. It is likely that the interrelationships both within and between such communities were based on kinship. Noted in comments by our brief Roman visitors as tribal societies, such communities survived into the later medieval period in both the clan system of the Highlands and the Border reiving families. In fact this pattern survived until relatively recently, as can be seen in General Roy's military maps of 1745–6 (NLS).

This remarkable cultural continuity was predicated on a deep, specific attachment to the local physical environment. Elsewhere, Stuart has written of how the visceral attachment to land in tribal societies defines and informs the ongoing processes of oral tradition (McHardy 2016: 45f). Stones of the Ancestors shows that such processes are inextricably intertwined with the concept of the ancestors. Put simply, individuals in these communities were raised not simply to revere their ancestors but to understand how they had paved the way for contemporary society to continue to survive. And that process depended on stories that referred not just to the ancestors, but to the landscape and the monuments that inhabited that landscape, monuments to the ancestors themselves.

Monuments, Measurement and Myth

When the first Ordnance Survey maps of Scotland were being created, the men charged with gathering evidence of place-names across the country relied on local informants. One of the results of this was that, on early maps such as OS 6-inch 1842–83, a great many ancient monuments were described as Pictish, sometimes with the form Pecht. There are Pictish roads, Pictish camps, Pictish Forts and Pictish Knowes from Shetland to the border with England. As subsequent scholarship has shown, the monuments so described are of varying antiquity, many of them long pre-dating what we have come to think of as the Pictish period of the 1st millennium AD. What this suggests is that to the population at large, whose ancestors had occupied the same landscape as them for millennia, the term Pict, or Pecht, meant something along the lines of 'the people who were here before us'. Another term for this is ancestors.

In the modern world, the term Pict has become limited to what is seen as a more detailed and informed understanding of the past. However, as we will show in this book, the ideas that come down through what is referred to as folklore in fact have a great deal to tell us, if carefully considered, and the idea of the Picts as the ancestor peoples of Scotland has much to recommend it. Defining the Pictish period in Scotland by external sources is not helpful. The suggestion that they were given their name by the Romans because of a habit of tattooing – for which there is no extant evidence – is intellectually risible. Tattooing was extremely common in this period even among Roman legionnaires. Likewise is the notion that the Pictish period begins with a reference to them in a Roman panegyric of 297. The first known written reference to the Picts is in what is believed to be a list of forts on the Antonine Wall that appears in the Ravenna Cosmography, an 8th century compilation of place-names covering the area from Ireland to India. The document drew on earlier written material including maps. The actual term in the list is Pexa, which according to the Roman specialists Rivet and Smith (Rivet and Smith 1979: 438) is not a place-name, but a tribal name. The Antonine Wall was abandoned in the 160s, so the name must predate that. The Roman writers upon whom we rely for our earliest reports referred to the indigenous peoples of what is now Scotland as both Caledonians and Picts.

However, as W.J.W. Watson pointed out (Watson 1926: 67–8), most of the neighbouring peoples of the Picts had names for them which were very like the term that survived in Scottish folklore, 'Pecht', and none of them had any word resembling 'Caledonian'. The idea that they were given the name Picti by those same Romans is to accord the Romans an importance in Scotland's history which is unjustifiable. In a recent article, Gordon Barclay (Barclay 2001) drew attention to the problems of analysing Scottish prehistory (and we suggest history), through a process that sees England as central and Scotland as peripheral (McHardy 2015). Nowhere is this more apparent than in the long-term attitude towards the Romans. Put at its simplest, England was a part of the Roman Empire for 400 years, while the longest occupation of any part of Scotland appears to have been on the Antonine Wall – for a period of less than 30 years – and this was a period of military occupation, not widespread Roman settlement. This is important because the basic human occupation pattern of most of Scotland that has been labelled 'fermtoun and clachan' survived from before the Roman invasions and lasted in much of the country until the 18th century. What this means is that local tradition, passed on from word to mouth, has the potential to have originated a very long time ago indeed.

Recent statistical analysis performed on story types at the University of Durham suggests that some of these stories are at least 5,000 years old (Tehrani 2016). There is now strong evidence that the Australian aboriginal stories have lasted for tens of millennia (Isaacs 1980 *passim*) and there is the potential for some story motifs being much older even than that (McHardy 2003). There has long been reluctance, often refusal, on the part of British archaeologists and historians alike to give any credence to folklore, on the grounds that such material can never be reliable, given the idea of Chinese whispers and a total lack of structure and control over the process of oral transmission, but a recent occurrence shows how misguided this is.

In a television documentary on the remarkable archaeological investigations taking place at the Ness of Brodgar on Orkney, one of the presenters, an engineer, inadvertently showed just how valuable folklore can be in enhancing our understanding of the past.

STENNESS STONE CIRCLE, ORKNEY, MOONRISE
HY 30672 12515 58° 59' 39" N 3° 12' 30" W

In this part of the programme, the question was raised – how did the local inhabitants move the great megaliths 5,000 years ago? After experimentation with wooden rollers and ropes had proved of limited success in moving a large stone, even with considerable numbers of helpers, a local man, Allan Tulloch, proprietor of the Standing Stones Hotel, stepped forward and said that he had been told that the best way to move the stones was by sliding them on seaweed. This was tried and it worked extremely well. Thousands of years after the creation of the various sites in the area, a key piece of technological knowledge was still retained locally and yet the programme made no reference to this notable example of information being passed down orally for millennia. The reality is that the majority of those who make their living from investigating the past have tended to treat folklore as if it is essentially childish, so ignoring a source of considerable potential value.

In this work we do not ignore folklore; in fact, we consider it to be an important tool to help us better understand the far past. Dougie's work on discerning the alignments of ancient monuments is set alongside Stuart's analysis of the landscapes they inhabit, part of the developing subject of Geomythography (McHardy 2016: 45f). Dougie's surveys and his unique photographic record illustrate how the construction of many of our ancient monuments involved alignments to the sun and moon at significant times of the year (something which continued to have relevance into the 1st millennium AD and on into Christian historical times). However, years of investigation have led him to conclude that no advanced mathematical or astronomical knowledge would have been required for the creation of these monuments.

We humans are prone to imagining (hoping) that there was a Golden Age in the far past, but the evidence is clear. Professor Alexander Thom opened up a great deal of necessary debate with his work on megalithic structures (Thom 1967, 1971). Although some monuments are egg shaped or have flattened facades, there are other simple methods of creating these shapes as opposed to the complex geometry proposed by Professor Thom. Archaeoastronomers learn if ancient monuments were aligned towards the sun and moon by surveying them with a theodolite using complex calculations. The general reader cannot understand this information and this was exacerbated by Thom reading too much into his highly accurate surveys. This is not to say that our ancestors could not count and there are examples of sophisticated hidden orientations built into monuments. All the builders had to do was simply to watch, mark and align the monument to where the sun or moon rose or set on the horizon around the time of their choosing.

We know that the islands scattered over thousands of miles of the Pacific Ocean were reached by people who were capable of navigating by the sun, moon and stars (Lewis 1978). Martin comments that the Western Isles fishermen knew that the complex motion of the tides was linked with the position and phases of the moon (Martin 1703: 44–7). This information would have been orally passed on to each succeeding generation, without any need for mathematical calculation. Dougie suggests that the archaeoastronomy surveys should only be used as a general guide to the times when the sun or moon will rise or set in line with the monuments. We believe that the alignments, which we show were in use in communally raised monuments over millennia, were essentially expressions of spiritual beliefs at the eight divisions of the year within an already established Neolithic calendar, rather than for scientific astronomy. This can be seen in the solar/lunar orientations of passage tombs scattered across the country, which in certain areas are expressed in different architectural forms. These monuments would also have acted as the focus for ritual activity involving the ancestors and the sun and moon, within these agricultural self-sufficient localised economies. Such small-scale, self-sufficient but interdependent communities, the norm in Scotland until just 300 years ago, provided a framework for the survival of long-term, traditional culture. The centrality of the importance of alignment can be seen from the earliest widespread, man-made structures we have in Scotland – chambered cairns – and continued to be important through the subsequent developments of later henges, stone circles and arrangements into historical times. This continuity is quite clear: the alignments were an ongoing central component in the development of those large and often complex megalithic sites, such as the Ness of Brodgar, Calanais and Kilmartin, which can be understood as extensive sacred landscapes. Over time, the style of monuments altered, for reasons that we can probably never know, but this centrality of solar and lunar alignment continued well into historical times, as this book shows. One point will recur time and again in this work and that is that the ancient monuments of Scotland, while in many cases conforming to a general type or pattern, are all unique. Each monument or group of monuments is different from all the others and this may well reflect something that we see in oral tradition itself, where widespread common story motifs are given a local provenance through being set within the visible environment of the community. In his studies into folklore, myth and legend, Stuart has become convinced that the academic pursuit of origin points for such material is an exercise in futility.

Stories survive within local environments by being located by the tellers within the known environment of the audience. Given what we know of settlement patterns in prehistory, the transfer of most forms of knowledge through the spoken word – a universal attribute of human culture before the invention of writing – can perhaps be best understood through consideration of how children learned. They were told stories, and for this method to have any true value the process would involve setting mythological and legendary material within the environment that the children knew. This means that in every tale of 'King' Arthur, of Finn MacCoul, or of the Cailleach we see the same relevance for the local community within whose culture the stories survived. The tales, like the monuments, are localised and belong to the culture of the local community; each version is securely located within its own social and physical environment. By this, we do not mean that every different clachan or fermtoun had a separate culture but that the shared aspects of the culture were localised within the known environment of the population, probably at a tribal level, though potentially even more locally concentrated.

The Monuments

While there is evidence of human activity in Scotland going back to 12000 BC, most of the earliest finds are middens from later periods and other evidence from essentially domestic sites. The first actual monuments do not begin to appear until the middle of the 4th millennium BC, with the beginning of the complex sites at Barnhouse, Ness of Brodgar on Orkney, the Cleaven Dyke at Meikleour in Perthshire and other sites in Argyll. Already these sites show significant solar alignments and this continued in later types of structures, such as chambered tombs and cairns and stone circles. Many of the surviving monuments from the Stone Age onwards, like the chambered tombs and cairns, are, at least partially, funerary. Many of the chambered tombs contain multiple burials, but not enough to suggest they were the burial sites of entire communities. Some form of selection must have existed of those to be enclosed in these structures, which were extremely time-consuming to build, but the simplistic idea that such chosen ones were members of some 'elite' within society is only one step away from the long-discredited notion that all such funerary structures were the burials of kings. What we can be sure of is that within the probable tribal societies which created them, there were different levels of status, but the idea that status and power must be inextricably linked within such societies is wishful thinking on the part of those who like to see all of human history as having been dominated by elites.

The very existence of the monuments themselves shows they were raised by communities at large and the idea that humans can only work together under the direction of leaders flies in the face of what we know of human society over the past few hundreds of thousands of years. It would seem likely that the tribal structures that survived in most of Scotland into the 2nd millennium AD, and much later in the Highlands and Lowlands, were descended from earlier forms of society following the same basic socio-economic pattern: fermtoun and clachan, in which the population lived in scattered, small, self-sufficient communities, was already around in the Stone Age and as General Roy's military maps clearly show, that pattern was still in existence over much of the country in the mid-18th century. The Clearances in both the Highlands and Lowlands, which have shaped our current landscape, effectively replaced a population pattern that was millennia old in many, if not most, parts of Scotland. Scotland's unfortunate history of absentee landlordism and elite exploitation is not really that old. Within the ancient kinship-based societies there were chieftains and others who had considerable status and power in these societies, but confusion arises with the conflation of status and power. Chiefs were undoubtedly powerful – their central role in any tribal system made them socio-political leaders and the arbiters of dispute – but alongside that they were the prime functionaries of the mutual support system that defines tribalism. That chiefs could be and sometimes were removed from their position by the people of their clan is well attested, as is the belief amongst everyday clan members that they were related to their chief (Burt 1998). To interpret the system of consanguinity that underpinned tribal arrangements around the world as being in any way feudal is simply wrong. Other clearly definable roles within the system, such as smiths and other metal workers, may well have had considerable status, but like the bards and healers (almost certainly women in earlier times), why would they have had power over others? The now discredited idea that all ancient monuments were the burial sites of high status individuals needs to be replaced by an understanding that the creation of these monuments was a group activity. The evidence suggests that for most of humanity's story in Scotland, this group was the tribe, or a section thereof. From the time of the chambered tombs onwards, we are seeing evidence of a regard for the dead, those who had gone before. We cannot be sure what the beliefs of the people who raised the first tombs were, but that there is respect for the ancestors is clear.

The surveys show that the light of the sun or moon entered the passage tombs and lined up with the rows of standing stones. We think that this, along with the ritual use of cup marks in Gaelic folklore, was when people believed they made contact with their ancestors to ask them to make their crops fruitful. It is probable the bones that were interred – the thigh and skull bones of numbers of individuals – could have been used in such rituals. In a remarkable suggestion of cultural continuity, Scottish gravestones from the 15th century and later have representations of skulls and thigh bones – which may well have been the origin of the well-known skull and crossbones motif associated with the modern Hollywood

INSCHFIELD RECUMBENT STONE CIRCLE, INSCH, ABERDEENSHIRE
NJ 62331 29349 Lat. 57° 21' 11" N Long. 2° 37' 40" W

Midwinter sunset at 2.42pm, 10 December 2017.

idea of pirates. Whether or not we can be sure of such activity, there can be no doubt that the very existence of the differing types of monuments that were raised in Scotland from the Stone Age onwards show us that at the very least there was some sort of reverence for the ancestors. Western anthropologists looking at societies elsewhere came up with the idea of 'ancestor worship', but it seems that this might be better understood not as worship but as respect, possibly reverence. After all those who had gone before had not only given life to the current generation, they had handed down the accumulated knowledge of the community that enabled the current generation to live within their environment. We know from folklore in many cultures that the idea of being able to interrelate with the ancestors was an integral part of folk belief and ritual well into the modern era.

Such reverence was fostered by the use of story, oral transmission having been the only means of passing on both knowledge and belief before the invention of writing, which is relatively recent in the human story. The idea of the ancestors as somehow still existing after death is again a common human idea and, well into historical times, some of this type of thinking seems to have pervaded what we know of the belief in fairies. In Scotland, the belief in fairies was widespread and equates with the ancestors. A very widely spread type of tale – known from all parts of Scotland – involves humans being lured into fairy mounds, some of which were ancient burial monuments, and dancing with the fairies, unaware of time passing. Sometimes the person – often a musician, which may suggest there is more to be learned from such tales given the role of music in so much human sacral behaviour – is rescued by a companion after a year and a day and in other instances returns after a hundred years to find that all has changed, their family has died and they in turn quickly fade away.

Such ideas are also linked to the again widespread story of a hero being buried with his companions in a significant hill or mound. These survive in stories of Finn McCoul and the Fianna within what were Gaelic-speaking areas in the past and those of Arthur and his knights in Scots-speaking areas that earlier had P-Celtic speaking populations, the best known of which is Arthur and the Picts asleep in Arthur's Seat in Edinburgh. A student of Stuart's actually remembered this story from her youth as being Arthur and the Pixies, which seems oddly apposite. In such tales, the great heroic figures can be seen as representative not just of the ancestors themselves, but of the continuity of culture that had been passed down through time. This linkage is reinforced by the association with both notable hills and mountains in the landscape and ancient monuments. Many such tales are linked specifically to *sithean*, a Gaelic word for a fairy mound, of which there are many across Scotland. These mounds have these stories attached to them despite the mistaken idea that such places are remnants of motte-and-bailey castles due to a supposed widespread Norman incursion into Scotland. Most of them are in fact prehistoric and appear to have had important social functions (McHardy 2012: 139ff). There is no doubt that fairy belief was complex and, as has been pointed out by Black (2004 *passim*), the stories themselves could be used to deal with misfortune and even criminal behaviour within small communities. Given the association of so many ancient monuments with fairy belief, we can assume that some at least of such beliefs are rooted in the distant past and in the notion of reverence for the ancestors.

In 1815, *The Secret Commonwealth of Elves, Fauns and Fairies* by the Reverend Robert Kirk of Aberfoyle (1644–92) was published. Kirk observes:

There be manie places called Fayrie hills, which the mountain-people think impious and dangerous to peel or discover, by taking earth or wood from them; superstitiously believing the souls of their predecessors to dwell yr [there]. And for that end (say they) a Mote or Mount was dedicated beside everie church-yard, to receave their souls, till their adjacent Bodies arise, and so become as a Fayrie hill. (Stewart, ed. 1991)

As a minister, Kirk was not only well-placed to know how people thought, he also seems to have been sympathetic to such ideas if not a believer in them himself.

That such ideas changed over time is inarguable. The idea that the fairies were originally inhabitants of heaven who left with Lucifer is clearly post-Christian. Underlying such beliefs were truly ancient ideas, as the link with ancient monuments itself suggests. It is also worth remembering, as noted above, that many of our ancient monuments recorded in the first Ordnance Survey maps were called Pictish. This was because the term Pictish was applied by local people to a remarkably wide range of monuments, from Shetland to the Borders, some dating from the Stone Age and, on one level, it seems that the very notion of the Picts, often in the Scots form Pecht in much of our folklore, was being used as a general term meaning the ancestors. The reverence for one's ancestors has not gone away, as the burgeoning interest in genealogy clearly shows. What can be understood through looking at the idea of the ancestors is that within indigenous culture – in all its varieties across the different parts of Scotland – there has always been a sense of continuity, a continuity that understood the present as having a community with the past.

The idea of spirits of the dead walking the land at Halloween/Samhain has apparently transmogrified into a fashionable obsession with zombies and the like, fostered by the film and television industry, but it has its roots deep in human culture across the globe. And there is significant evidence that some of the rituals that still take place at various sites today are part of a continuity with the far past that folklore continues to reflect. The truth of the matter is that traditional stories survive within communities because they have relevance for both audience and teller. Although in today's world there is a tendency to think of storytelling as simple entertainment, its roots are in preserving a living culture within the community and, to a considerable extent, doing so in communion with the past. British archaeologists have tended to dismiss folklore as having little use in understanding the past simply because they are not concerned with dateable, provable reality. Human actions – individual, communal and societal – are not always driven by matters of provable fact. Culture depends on a wide range of assumptions, beliefs, knowledge and perception and an example of that complexity can be seen in the reverence for the ancestors which the evidence suggests was an integral part of the ideas behind the construction of our ancient monuments.

Types of Monuments

Communities started building large-scale monuments in Scotland around 5,500 years ago. The earliest signs of human occupation date back to 12000 BC with a scatter of flints at Elsrickle, near Biggar. Various limited settlement evidence from a range of locations exists over the next few millennia until the oldest house, at South Queensferry, dated at around 8400 BC. We have no monuments from this early in Scotland, but it seems likely people used ritual spaces from the earliest times. This idea is supported by the finds at Gobekli Tepe in Anatolia, part of modern Turkey, where a complex site of sculpted and carved stones was raised in the period 7560–7350 BC, on a site which has evidence of human activity from over a thousand years earlier (Gobekli). The point here is that megalithic structures were raised in a period that archaeologists believe was before the development of human settlement in this area, so the possibility exists that some 'sacred sites' could pre-date settled culture here in the British Isles.

What triggered the erection of large-scale monuments here is, and will probably remain, unclear. It appears likely that the initial idea for raising such labour-intensive structures came from elsewhere, perhaps Brittany, where the earliest Western European megalithic structures have been dated to circa 5000 BC. A thousand years before that, there is evidence of megalithic construction in Portugal. From the very beginning, the need was clear for solar and lunar alignments to be inbuilt to the construction of our ancient monuments.

Other significant early sites include the massive oval-shaped timber structure of Woodhenge in Wiltshire in southern England, dating from circa 2300 BC, which is generally accepted to be aligned to the midsummer sunrise. However, the surveys suggest it is aligned to the northern and southern rising and setting major standstill moon. The most outstanding example of a solar/lunar aligned monument is undoubtedly Stonehenge in the south of England and there has been much discussion of how it was used as an observatory. However, the cremated bone in the 56 Aubrey Holes and the orientation of the Heel Stone suggest that originally it was a burial monument aligned to the midsummer sunrise.

Surveys of the oldest Knap of Howar house on the Orkney island of Papa Westray show that it was aligned to the setting sun in early May and August. He also found similar solar and lunar alignments have been noted at the buildings at Barnhouse and at the Ness of Brodgar on Orkney. House 2 at Barnhouse was described as a cross between a house and a burial cairn, as it had a burial placed near its centre in line with the entrance (Richards 2013: 82–83). The entrance passage was aligned to where the southern moon would rise every 19–20 years during its minor standstill. The solar/lunar orientations of these monuments have a funerary or ritual aspect to them, which can also be seen at the magnificent and diverse sites of Brodgar, Calanais and Kilmartin, which were preceded by structures which were both complex and sophisticated. Although many solar/lunar aligned monuments show signs that they were used for the dead, others – such as the Nether Largie and Comet Stones in Argyll and on Orkney – do not. It is recognised that this might be due to such sites not yet being archaeologically investigated.

The 3km-long Cleaven Dyke in Perthshire is dated to circa 3600 BC. Its possible orientation to the sunrise and sunset in early November and May was assessed by Ruggles, who said that it was not aligned to the sun at these times (Barclay, Maxwell 1998: 50). However, the surveys and photographs confirmed that the Dyke was aligned to the sun at these times. The creation of the Cleaven Dyke would have required thousands of hours of human labour. It remains a puzzle as to whether this was done by a small local community, or group of

COPY OF THE WESTRAY WIFIE, ORKNEY

communities at a tribal level, working together over time, or perhaps the coming together of a larger population from a very wide area.

Such an idea would suggest some sort of complex and widespread organised social structure. The former seems the more likely and fits well with modern interpretations that see what were previously considered hill-forts to be instead sites of varied communal social activity that may well have included ritual behaviour. This does not rule out some such structures having had a defensive purpose at some time during their existence, only that it precludes this being their essential purpose. The earliest date so far from the site at Brodgar is 3500 BC, which matches that for the first activity at the complex site on Cairnpapple Hill in West Lothian. Both of these were sites of activity for at least 1,000 years but, as folklore indicates, their relevance in the culture of the local indigenous people continued into the modern era. By the time these sites fell out of use, monumental fashion had changed and, at Cairnpapple, there is clear evidence of a henge monument.

Henge monuments start to appear around 3200 BC and the Stones of Stenness, which are part of the same sacred landscape as the Brodgar complex, were built during this time. Shortly after this, the landscape at Kilmartin in Argyll began to be developed and stone circles started to be built here and elsewhere for the next 1,000 years. One particular find from Links of Noltland on the Orkney island of Westray, which is putatively dated to between 3000 and 2500 BC, is the small figurine known as the Westray Wifie (Wife). Apart from its obvious femininity, linking it to the widespread folklore motif of the Cailleach in Gaelic and the Carlin in Scots, a potential Mother Goddess-type figure, this and a similar figure from Skara Brae clearly show that the idea of representational art was around in what we now call Scotland, far back in prehistory. Leaving aside how this relates to the vast amounts of cup and-ring and related rock art, it should also be noted that the Ballochmyle rock art site, dated to mid-3rd millennium BC, has clear representations of three deer. Other similar figures at Glen Domhain, Kilmartin and on Black Hill in Edinburgh are sometimes reckoned to be modern, but the Westray Wifie and its companion piece, the Brodgar Boy (Brodgar), as well as the Ballochmyle deer, are indisputable evidence that representational art was part of the indigenous culture in prehistoric times. On the southern section of the northern Ballochmyle wall, there is what could be interpreted as a human representation – perhaps, like the Westray Wife, a Goddess.

Another significant human representation is the wooden figure of the Ballachulish Goddess, which is dated circa 600 BC. This carved figure was found covered with some wicker matting in a bog and outside the village of Ballachulish on the northern shore of Loch Leven in 1880. A photograph of the Ballachulish Goddess was taken before she dried out and her shrunken figure is now on display in the Museum of Scotland in Edinburgh. Other wood and stone, male and female fertility figures have been found in other parts of the British Isles from the Bronze Age to the early medieval Sheela na gigs in Ireland. From the few wooden figures that have survived, it is likely that during the prehistoric period they numbered in their thousands. In light of the dating attributed to the Pictish Symbol Stones, this has great significance, as we shall see later. From about 3000 BC, we see the creation of chambered tombs in various parts of Scotland. While the limitations of early antiquarianism can be seen in the idea that these were the tombs of 'high status individuals', our knowledge of them has increased. It is now known that these were communal burial sites. The surviving bones found, usually skulls and thigh bones, clearly come from a range of individuals, but the method of selection of those to be interred is and will probably remain unclear. What we can say is that, along with all the other large-scale monuments, they could only have been constructed by communal activity, while their role in representing those who had gone before – the ancestors – appears absolutely central to their being built.

Given that we know so little about the specifics of the local kinship and socio-economic structures at the various sites where chambered tombs were erected, we must be aware that there is a range of possibilities of how such selection occurred. What we do know about how society developed here in Scotland is that the underlying structure of tribalism continued to be the norm for much of the population even into the 18th century, though we must always take care not to impose anachronistic ideas on the past. As noted elsewhere (Barclay 2001), Scottish prehistory has been bedevilled by attempting to fit it into narratives developed for elsewhere and, just as

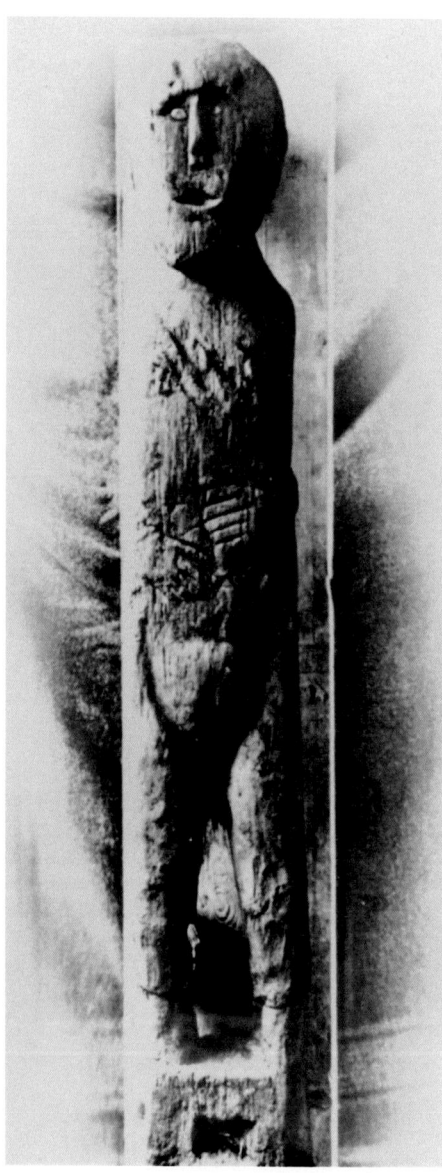

BALLACHULISH GODDESS, LOCH ETIVE, ARGYLL
NN 05607 60124 56° 41' 32" N 5° 10' 34" W

Courtesy of HES (Society of Antiquaries Scotland)

folklore preserves what people told each other about the past, so we must remember that underlying the Scottish tribal (clan) system was the basic idea that all members of the tribe were related. Ideas of status and power developed in different societies do not and will not fit. The chambered tombs range over times and styles and, in Scottish terms, the main concentrations are the over 600 Clyde Cairns stretching from the Solway Forth to the Isle of Mull and, in the north east, from the Moray Firth to the Orkneys and divided into four main groupings, Clava, Orkney-Cromarty and the Maeshowe and Shetland and Hebridean groupings. There are subdivisions within the Clyde Cairns group such as the Bargrennan group.

But the general stylistic continuity is remarkable in the extent to which its area overlaps with the historical 'kingdom' of Strathclyde – a proto-nation state of the P-Celtic speaking Britons, a confederation of tribes that require considerable further investigation. It is tempting to see another division into tribal or tribal-confederation based polities or societies in the different monument types of the north-western monuments. Given that there are provable continuities in the socio-economic patterns of fermtoun and clachan from at least the period known as the Iron Age (from around 1500 BC), we are perhaps justified in suggesting that there are continuities, not just of belief, but perhaps of identity. As with the oldest of our stories, each of these monuments became further localised in its relationship not just to the landscape but to the people who inhabited that landscape. The suggestion that has been made of the possible existence of 'specialist monument-builders' and such groupings might be thus interpreted as being themselves specifically attached to such tribal or tribal confederations structures.

At the risk of belabouring the point, Barclay's analysis of the problems of Core and Periphery suggests that we should be considering such evidence within its own local and supra-local areas rather than attempting to fit it to patterns developed by the analysis of sites elsewhere. While analysis with contemporaneous sites from other cultures and locales is a standard archaeological approach, the process of looking at monuments as part of local cultural continuity has much to recommend it and is an integral part of the Geomythographical approach Stuart is developing. The aforementioned instance of the process for moving megaliths on Orkney is a case in point. There, despite extensive economic, linguistic, social, religious and political change, a truly ancient, useful piece of data survived within the oral tradition of the local community.

Dougie has spent many years investigating not only the Orkney-Cromarty cairns, but also the Clava type passage cairns located around Inverness, which can be seen as examples of how fashions in monuments not only changed but remained essentially localised. The Clava Cairns are thought to have been raised in the early Bronze Age and examples of their specific type of chambered cairn construction are all found within a radius of 30 miles from Balnuaran of Clava. There are many different alignments built into the construction of this site and all or most of them correspond to the pattern of the eightfold division of the year. George Bain was the first person to try to assess the central Clava ring cairn for possible solar alignments and, while he found that one stone marked the equinox sunrise, his surveys of the other stones were well off their targets (Bain 1886–7: 122).

The stone rows have been seen as focusing near specific dates, or more properly, times of the year. But as they have been found with the dead, this suggests that they are another type of sacred burial monument. Rather than being used for astronomy, perhaps we should think of the monuments being sacred to the sun, moon and the ancestors. Even the much discussed light-box effect at Newgrange in Ireland, where the sun shone through a gap above the entrance to illuminate a carved stone in the central chamber, is not seen just on the day of the midwinter solstice. The effect lasted for a couple days either side of the solstice – and this is the pattern of alignments everywhere. They are not precisely calculated or created to a specific time on a specific day. Their practicality rests on them being of use to the community as markers of the eight divisions of the year. As reflected in the folklore, this could have been seen as a symbolic impregnation of the earth by the sun. The surveys illustrate that the monuments were aligned to near the winter and summer solstices (the shortest and longest days of the year), the vernal and autumnal equinoxes (when the days and nights are the same length) and the feast days of the old agricultural calendar (Scott, D. 2012, 2016). These survive in Scotland and Ireland in the Gaelic forms of their names, as Bride or Imbolc on 1 February, Beltane on 1 May, Lughnasad (Lammas) on 1 August and Samhain (Halloween) on 1 November.

These times were significant in the agricultural year. Imbolc was when the first lambs would be born, meaning that after the hardship of the dark winter months there would now be access to milk and its products, something that was invaluable for children and adults alike. 1 May is often seen as a kind of New Year, when the cattle were taken from the houses and sent off to pasture away from the planted crops around the fermtouns and clachans. Lughnasad was when the harvest began, a time of fulfilment after the labours of the year. Samhain was the time of readying for winter, when all but brood cattle would be slaughtered and laid down for the coming months. This created a basic solar pattern of a significant date roughly every 45 days. A number of sites focus on the moon's major and minor standstills – the times when moonrise or moonset occurs near its most northerly and southern points, about every 19–20 years. The major standstill is when the moon will rise and set beyond the sun's summer and winter solstice positions – monuments such as Nether Largie and Calanais are aligned to the moon at this time. The minor standstill is when the moon's northern and southern limits are restricted within those of the solstices and this occurs about nine years after a major standstill. While over the past couple of decades, the centrality of alignments in the location and construction of ancient monuments has been increasingly understood, problems do arise. Many people accepted that Maeshowe on Orkney was aligned to allow the midwinter sunlight to shine along its passage into the central burial chamber. Dougie's research has shown that as an outer part of the passage was removed in the 1860s, the sunlight shining through the original low outer entrance would only have reached about halfway along the passage. Just as we have to be critical of the folklore that has survived down millennia, so we must always be careful to check what archaeology and archaeoastronomy has already accepted of the sites under investigation. It is worth noting that the name Maeshowe translates directly from Scots, the indigenous Germanic language of Scotland that is still widely spoken, to Maiden's or Maidens' Mound. The term 'maiden' has many connotations, not just of fertility but of ritual and belief (McHardy 2012: 130 and McNeil 1959: v 2p 120ff).

From around 2700 BC another significant type

of monument begins to appear, stone circles and henges, which are found over a wide geographical area reaching far beyond Scotland. It is believed that many such circles may have been preceded by similar structures formed with wooden posts. Henges are monuments which have central areas defined by external ditches and often, as at Ring of Brodgar, contain circles of stone. It is clear from the evidence that these monuments were raised as defined areas, separate from the rest of the landscape and thus, were most likely the focus of rituals that were enacted on the days that correspond to the alignments built into their construction. While many circles, like Stenness and Brodgar, are generally similar to others elsewhere, a distinctive localised style arose in Aberdeenshire in north-east Scotland. These are the recumbent stone circles, where a large horizontal stone is flanked by two uprights, and there is some evidence to suggest they may have developed from other monuments such as the Clava Cairns.

The kerbstones and long axis of some Clava cairns are graded in height towards large kerbstones that look like false portals and are mainly placed towards the rising and setting midwinter sun (Scott, D. 2016). These false portals are similar to the false portalled kerb cairns in Perthshire and Argyll and the recumbent stone circles which are also placed in line with the sun or moon. While the recumbent stone circles are limited to north-east Scotland, there are similar circles in south-west Ireland, but these and the others in Scotland are likely to have been influenced by the large recumbent stone in front of the midwinter aligned passage of Newgrange in Ireland. The passage of Carn Bann and the Kintraw and Culcharron false portals in Argyll are aligned to the midwinter sun, while those at Strontoiler in Argyll and Lochbuie on Mull are aligned towards the rising major and minor standstill moon. These ideas would have gradually spread by land or sea, reminding us that this kind of travel in distant prehistory was much more prevalent than used to be thought. This would also explain the cultural connections between the monuments such as Calanais on Lewis and the Ring of Brodgar on Orkney, believed to have been erected circa 2500 BC. A safer route between Ireland and Orkney was from Argyll up through the Great Glen and along the east coast of Sutherland and Caithness. This is shown from the surveys of the solar/lunar aligned monuments in Argyll, the Clava Cairns around Inverness and the Orkney-Cromarty passage cairns scattered along the east coasts of the Sutherland and Caithness (Scott, D. 2016).

What is clear is that the locations of the monuments were very carefully chosen to maximise the use of the height of the surrounding horizon in their solar/lunar orientations. This means that there must have been someone with the skill to find such positions in the landscape. The continuance of monument building and ritual behaviour associated with the ancestors and the sun and moon at such sites reflect a continuum of importance to the local community that could only strengthen over time. We may never know precisely why such sites were chosen but their ongoing relevance to their communities is reflected in folklore as well as the respect shown to them by their communities into the modern era. Such changes in monumental style is proof that the continuities of usage of sites that had been of importance in the past was common, if not in fact universal. Because of how we inhabit the modern world, it is all too easy for us to forget that our ancestors, both distant and more recent, inhabited their environments differently than we do. They were much more directly attached to their physical environments in cultural ways that we have lost and, though there is evidence for considerable long-range sea travel, the majority of the inhabitants of these islands from the earliest times through to relatively modern times would have been unlikely to travel more than a few days' walk from where they lived.

In Scotland, with the survival of basic occupation patterns and the lack of major urban environments, this would have been particularly the case. It is this attachment to the land itself, visceral rather than intellectual, that underpinned the relationship between local populations and those monuments whose very existence was a constant reminder of their own continuity with their direct ancestors and the past of the landscape itself, rooted in both the monuments and oral tradition. Standing stones are found in much of the country and their dating can be problematic. Alison Sheridan has dated standing stones in the Kilmartin Glen to 1300 BC (Sheridan 2012: 180). Perhaps other standing stones belong to this period? Single stones such as the Watch and Odin Stones on Orkney are known to have had companion stones, the stump and stone holes of which were found through excavations. Other stones known as outliers are also linked to stone circles.

Professor Thom was the first to show from the Temple Wood stone circle that the Nether Largie stones in the Kilmartin Glen were aligned to the rising sun at midwinter, the winter quarter times in early November and February and to the moon during the major and minor lunar standstills (Thom 1967, 1971). Aubrey Burl found and excavated the stump of standing stones some 260m south of the southern Temple Wood circle. When this stone (S7) was surveyed by Jon Patrick from the centre of the circle, it was found to be indicating where the southern major standstill moon set on Bellanoch Hill (Hawkin 1984: 98, 101–2). The 1991 surveys found that, from the central Nether Largie stone, the equinox sun set above Stone 7. The axis between the Temple Wood stone circles was aligned to the northern rising moon and the setting midwinter sun (Scott, D. 2012). It is also the case that a great many standing stones have one or more cup marks, reflecting the reality that working stone is of great antiquity in Scotland. Cup marks on solar/lunar aligned Ballymeanoch standing stones and those at Nether Largie near Kilmartin were probably quarried from nearby carved outcrops. However, although the large broad Ballymeanoch stone is heavily cup marked on its eastern side, the two faint cup marks on its lower western side could have been carved after the stone was raised. From the northern Temple Wood circle, the midwinter sun will set in line with the larger southern circle, which has a large double spiral carved on one of its northern stones (Scott, D. 2012). Recent surveys of spirals at Drumtroddan and Cauldside Burn in Galloway have also shown that they were aligned to the midwinter and the midsummer sun. It is obvious that such a link with spirals and the midwinter sun was widespread and these are very similar to those carved on Newgrange in Ireland. While we can never be sure whether the carvings on standing stones are contemporaneous with their erection, the combination of locating and raising such monuments and decorating them is one that lasted over considerable time.

Recently, Stuart has been investigating hilltop sites which refer directly to the Cailleach, originally a goddess figure (McHardy 2012: 124ff), which reflect the communal importance of these places. We should also remember that symbolism used on Iron Age jewellery and weaponry regularly used spiral motifs which have long been understood as having a solar significance. Monumental styles changed over time and different locales became the focus of communal, ritual activity but the re-use of carving symbols of the sun and moon on solar/lunar aligned Bronze Age monuments by the Picts, such as at Aberlemno and Edderton, suggest that the underlying cosmology of the people inhabiting what we now call Scotland did not undergo significant change until the arrival of Christianity. This indigenous linkage strongly suggests that the dating of the earliest (Class 1) Pictish Symbol Stones, predicated on supposed similarities with other non-indigenous carvings on stone, is in considerable need of being revisited.

The symbol stone near Collessie, to take another example, has a figure very like warriors described by Dio Cassius at the dawn of the 3rd century. The idea that representational art only came into Scotland after the arrival of the Romans is demonstrably unsustainable (Dio 1927: 264–5). The calendric importance of the chambered tombs, the megaliths and later constructions is echoed well into historical times. In 664, Bishop Wilfrid of Northumbria called together Christian practitioners from all over the British Isles to the Synod of Whitby. This was partially to deal with the reality that, by using slightly different calendars, the indigenous British Church and the Church of Rome were now celebrating Easter not just days but sometimes weeks apart. This was duly rationalised and the imposition of the Roman way soon diminished the power and obtained the land of the indigenous Church. In earlier times, there were no external authorities and each community, local or tribal, had to figure out its own relationship with time, therefore we cannot rule out the possibility that this was of as great significance to the monument builders as their apparent wish to acknowledge their ancestors. Whoever supervised the creation of the monuments it is certain that the understanding of the need to have some sort of calendar long preceded the raising of the monuments and was an established aspect of human culture when humans began arriving in these islands after the Ice Age. Even as the monuments became locally stylised, they continued to reflect ideas that were already long established in many other places.

The Builders

While it is clear that the construction of the monuments under consideration must have been undertaken by local communities, we must consider who designed and organised these efforts. It seems extremely unlikely that the skills and knowledge required for this would have been common enough for there to have been a specialist of this kind in every community. Perhaps we should think of there being specialists, or groups of specialists existing as part of overall tribal structure, perhaps a bit like the muinntir communities of early Christian monks attached to specific tribes or clans in Ireland and Scotland. This sort of specialisation might account for such localised monument styles as the Clava Cairns or the recumbent stone circles. An alternative explanation might be that there were peripatetic groups of such people akin in their interrelationship with the various communities to the metal-smiths and tinkers of much later times. In both cases, however, there is a problem. Even with the extensive number of ancient monuments built over time in Scotland (and elsewhere), it would appear unlikely that such groups would have this role and no other. Given that most monuments are clearly funerary, we can surmise that the builders could have been something akin to a priesthood, whose role might be better interpreted with reference to shamanic traditions, rather than the hierarchies of centralised religions. The term used by many commentators over the years is, of course, Druids.

Although the idea of the white-robed, long-bearded, venerable magicians of popular imagination is fanciful, there is some evidence for there having been some kind of Druidic presence in prehistoric north-western Europe. The problem is that so much written about the Druids comes from long after they had disappeared and the original references are remarkably few in number. Any Scottish references are late indeed and in this we see part of a wider problem. The extant literary sources from both Ireland and Wales that are taken to represent pre-Christian societies are in themselves problematic. While there is no doubt that the underlying stories behind the Irish sagas and the Welsh Mabinogion tales arose from extant oral traditions, the process of their being written down changed them. This is because those writing them down – Christian monks – not only had a world view based on the absolute rectitude and supremacy of their own religion, but were educated through processes that relied on the Bible and Classical Greek and Roman literature. They are effectively literary works and as such were designed 'to preach to the converted'. The 11th century Irish *Lebor Gabála Érenn* – generally translated as 'The Book of Invasions', though a tradition-bearer from Connemara recently told Stuart that a better translation might be 'The Book of Coming Together' – contains the following reference:

> Thereafter, the progeny of Bethach, Iarbonel the Soothsayer and Nemed were in the northern islands of the world, learning Druidry, knowledge, prophecy and magic, until they were expert in the arts of pagan cunning (*Lebor Gabála Érenn*, 304).

This is interesting in its reference to the northern islands. Given that this is a historical reference, it is likely to have originated before Iceland had been settled in the late 9th century AD. And given the close cultural ties between Ireland and the Hebrides stretching back into the far past, this reference could well be to Orkney, as Shetland – even farther north – does not have many ancient monuments. For many years, the influence of Irish culture on Scotland was overestimated (Campbell 2001) and there is little evidence of the early Irish mythological Tuatha dé Danann in place-names or surviving stories in Scotland, but to deny close similarities in both megalithic structures, folklore and other cultural areas between both areas would be silly. However, it is a fallacy to believe that, once literature appears, traditional storytelling disappears. For centuries after the original Irish and Welsh material was put onto paper (originally vellum) the majority of the populations of these countries continued to be illiterate and, despite the blandishments of Christian priests and later ministers, the stories continued to be told. This can be seen in Bishop Carswell's fulminations against local people preferring to listen to the old tales of the Tuatha dé Danann rather than the Bible. We also know that people continue to tell stories despite being formally educated. Certain Scottish storytellers today, whose family tradition involves of passing stories down through the generations, tell stories whose authenticity appears unassailable. Some of this material has never been in print. The incident mentioned at the beginning of this book where a local passed on knowledge of how the Orkney megaliths were moved is an example of how oral tradition can hold on to information within communities. We should remember that the Australian Diprotodon stories (Isaacs 1991), which are over 30,000 years old, are possibly not even the oldest stories still extant.

STONEHEAD RECUMBENT STONE CIRCLE, INCH, ABERDEENSHIRE

Midwinter sunset at 2.10pm, 10 December 2017.

Although the idea of the Druids has taken a firm hold on the popular imagination over the past few centuries, we must be careful not to rely on limited source material to suggest that the Druids raised any of the monuments we are considering. However, it does seem likely that some sort of specialised group must have been involved for the same fundamental patterns of monuments to have been raised over such a wide area. Some of the monuments were so big – the White Caterthun in Angus is a case in point – that the limited local populations must have taken generations of locals to build them. Communal activity on this scale must have required a degree of organisation that relied on a group of specialists, or possibly a single individual, accepted within local society. This in turn raises the possibility that there may have been schools of instruction for such practitioners where such massive and complicated projects could be discussed and planned. This is not to suggest that there was an organised or centralised religious structure, but that the disparate groups were, to use a modern religious analogy, 'singing from the same hymn book'.

Colin Richard made a valid point in addressing this. As a starting point it should be noted that concepts of order are inevitably cosmologically based: cosmologies allow a particular cultural understanding and categorisation of the lived and experienced world; they represent a way of 'thinking about' the multiplicity of images and experiences of individuals. In this sense, they are not simply abstractions but structure daily practices and perceptions of space and time: they are as real as people's lives. Cosmology is, therefore, necessarily embedded in the natural topography and environment (Tilley 1994) and through the categorisation of space and time particular natural places are recognised and images of landscape and order are created. (Richards 1966: 4). While it seems certain that the ideas underpinning the use of solar and lunar alignments were extant before people moved into north-western Europe after the end of the last Ice Age, it is also undeniable that each monument or group of monuments is unique. There may well have been general ideas of how such monuments should be created but the actual building of them all reflects a unique and localised approach. This corresponds remarkably with how tales, either mythological, legendary or other types of folklore, are set within the known landscape of the localised audience (McHardy 2003).

Stuart's work on the Nine Maidens groups of prehistory has come up with a variety of legendary and mythical groups of such women across most of north-western Europe and throughout the world, who certainly appear to have been specialist religious practitioners. One such group was mentioned in the 2nd century AD as being on the Isle de Sein off the Brittany coast and the island has become known as L'Isle des Druidesses. It is surely worth considering the possibility that, in periods where there seems to have been considerable focus on the idea of a Mother Goddess (Gimbutas 1991; McHardy 2012), ritual and sacred functions in such societies could have been carried out by women, particularly in light of the reported association of such groups with healing, divining and shape-shifting. It is perhaps telling that St Patrick is said to have driven off such a group from a well that subsequently bore his name (Harmon 2002: 156).

In locations such as Brodgar, Calanais, Kilmartin, Newgrange, the Boyne group, Avebury, Stonehenge and Carnac, the amount of effort involved in the design and creation of these complex structures suggests that such groups, if they did exist, may well have communicated with each other. The suggested number of people present at the decommissioning of structure 10 on the Ness of Brodgar circa 3000 BC was in the thousands (Feast) and this must have involved individuals from a great many different tribes or communities, given the population densities of north-western Europe at the time. To consider these specialists as an elite group is not necessarily helpful as we have no proof that status equalled power in such societies.

Smiths were always of high status in all metalworking societies but that does not mean they had control over anyone else, which is what reference to elites is generally suggestive of. The creation of monuments must have been communal and, without specific proof, the idea of a controlling elite is an assumption and a self-serving one at that. In all supposedly 'advanced' societies, education is predicated on literacy. In the human story this is a relatively recent development. For most of our species' time on the planet, the transmission of knowledge through oral transmission was the norm.

Julius Caesar mentions that the Druids trained for as long as 20 years and that they did write, and believed in reincarnation. He tells us, using the Greek alphabet, but suggests that their core beliefs were never written down. This can be understood as retaining not just the ideas they had inherited from their ancestors but also the methodology of remembrance and how it should be passed on. Significantly he also tells us:

> They likewise discuss and impart to the youth many things respecting the stars and their motion, respecting the extent of the world and of our earth, respecting the power and majesty of the immortal gods.

This clearly corresponds to what we would think of as specialists, though we have no clear idea as yet of how they were directly related to local communities.

The changeover to new types of monuments that coincided with the dawn of the Bronze Age may be due to new ideas penetrating such communities, brought in by newly arrived immigrants from Mainland Europe, for which there is some evidence (Migration). New techniques of building monuments may well have been something they brought with them. This is not to suggest that the incomers became dominant but merely that traditional societies, though conservative and rooted in ancestral and traditional practices and ideas, appear to have had the capacity to adapt to new ideas, as is clearly shown in the changing patterns of monument construction over time. The changing pattern of tool use from stone to bronze to iron is another case in point, though whether this was due to visitors bringing in new ideas and practices, or travellers going elsewhere and picking up new ideas, is and will remain moot.

A tantalising glimpse of the possibility of contact between such specialist practitioners comes from the Greek historian Herodotus, writing in the 5th century BC. He mentions a priest called Abaris coming to Greece from Hyperborea and meeting Pythagoras. Hyperborea, the land beyond the north wind, has been thought by many to refer to north-western Europe and possibly even more specifically the British Isles. Abaris is said to have come from the round or winged temple of Apollo (translations vary) in Hyperborea and this seems likely to refer to some sort of megalithic complex.

Given the size and complexity of the site at Ness of Brodgar and its potential role in the development of megalithic culture, and in light of our growing awareness of the sea as a highway rather than a barrier in prehistoric times, this potential link with Greece is not impossible. Herodotus also mentions that there was regular communication between the Oracle at Delphi and Hyperborea (Herodotus). Whether the specialists involved in the creation of the great monuments of the past were also what we might think of as shamans or priests, male and female, is unclear, but the discipline required to become a ritual practitioner on behalf of the group must have been considerable. Although, as Dougie points out, there was no need for advanced geometry or astronomy to create the various forms of monument that developed over time, they do appear to be too complex to have been raised by the population at large. There is a level of sophistication built into some monuments which could only have been accomplished by people with a high awareness of the movements of the sun and moon. All they had to do was to simply watch and build the monuments around markers indicating where the sun and moon rose or set on the horizon near the eight divisions of the year and the major and minor standstills every 20 years. We should try to understand that when building their burial monuments, our ancestors were perhaps using knowledge that had been in use for millennia.

Professor Thom has claimed that many of the shapes of some stone circles were created using Pythagorean geometry, but this was difficult to test. There is no doubt that these circles were laid out with simple geometry, but aerial photographs show that these flattened shapes could be simply created by scribing a large arc across the axis of a circle. The egg-shaped circles could have been easily made by joining two different sized circles. Many people still believe in Thom's high accuracy astronomy and this is perhaps a reluctance to adjust to, or ignorance of, the new information. As Richards pointed out, such constructions required a cosmological understanding of the world. In all human societies, the retention and development of such ideas has always been a specialist function. Everybody may have shared the same world view, but this had to be learned and this process would have been primarily through the spoken word. As most education was done through story, we see in this a bardic tradition that survived in the tradition of the seannachie in Scotland and that has long been seen as a significant part of Druidic tradition in the modern world.

The idea that the constructors of the megaliths and later monuments were dedicated single-function specialists does seem unlikely but that they were part of a specialised section of the populace, whether at a tribal or a supra-tribal level, seems indisputable. To subsequent generations, they would also be part of the ancestors. The association of so many monuments with mythical and legendary figures is part and parcel of the underlying cosmology of earlier societies and is itself reflective of the ongoing relevance of ideas transmitted through oral tradition. How much credence can be given to the tradition noted by Otta Swire (Swire 1996: 22) that the Calanais stones were raised by 'priests' who came in on ships and subsequently left is unclear, but we can be relatively certain that, if this did in fact occur, the 'priests' would have had the same cosmological beliefs as the local population, who were perhaps simply too few in number to support sufficient 'specialists' to undertake such work.

Alignments and the Power of the Sun

Solar alignments are associated with virtually all of our ancient monuments, from the earliest tombs through to at least some of the Pictish symbol stones. Tombs are often directed towards midwinter sunrises – the best known of these being Newgrange in Ireland – and the concept of light shining into the darkest recesses of a tomb over the midwinter solstice period is well attested. The finding that many ancient monuments were aligned to the sun has led to the theory that such alignments were used in a form of scientific astronomy. However, this is purely speculative. That there was veneration for the sun and, perhaps to a lesser extent, the moon, is demonstrated by the surveys in Part 2. There seems to be no doubt that the monuments were sites of ritual activity, sometimes continuing into historical times. The cosmology or world view of the people who raised the monuments is expressed in the monuments themselves, with reverence both for the ancestors and the power of the sun. Just as the monuments fit into the landscape, so the alignments locate them into the calendar at one or other of the eight significant divisions of the year.

The idea that some monuments, particularly the stone circles of the Bronze Age, were constructed using advanced geometry and astronomical techniques has not stood the test of time. But the relation of ancient monuments to the movements of the sun and moon *does* signify the application of a calendar – in other words, a measurable approach to time. In practical terms alone, in Scotland our weather is notoriously fickle and the creation of a physical marker that allows knowledge of the time of the year was of great significance. Even if the weather in the Bronze Age was warmer and clearer than today, the practical usefulness of this aspect of monument construction was something else that was inherited from the ancestors by later peoples.

From his research into Scottish and Irish Gaelic folklore, Dougie suggests that people may have believed that when the sun or moon lined up with the monuments, they 'energised' the spirit ancestors and that these spirits were the Sidhe, Sith, or the Tuatha dé Danann, who were thought to live in cairns and in standing stones. He proposes that these spirits are what we call the ancestors.

In Gaelic folklore, Ossian enters a burial cairn to talk with the Sidhe; similarly, the Ulster warrior Cú Chulainn meets women of the Sidhe after falling asleep while touching a standing stone. These metaphors of journeying to or making contact with the inhabitants of the Otherworld of Tír na nÓg, the Land of the Ever Young, are likely to reflect the beliefs of the Neolithic and Bronze Age. In the 12th century Irish Book of Armagh, these supernatural spirits were also called the Dei Terrani, or earth, or fertility gods. Martin Martin, writing in the late 17th century, comments that the people of the Hebrides believed that the light of the moon shining on the crops increased their vitality. This concern with fertility is something that Stuart's work on the Scottish supernatural females or goddesses, the Cailleach and the Carlin, supports.

This linkage of homage to the ancestors through the monuments, fertility and the power of the sun and the moon, lasted a very long time and provides a template for trying to understand the cosmology or world view of our predecessors. The choice of dates for the alignments on which the monuments were designed goes beyond the four main dates of the winter and summer solstices or the spring and autumnal equinoxes. The orientations to near the equinoxes were unlikely to be attempts to exactly define these times, and were perhaps just roughly marking the sun's position about halfway between the solstices. The other days, which were of importance in earlier times and which appear in the alignments, were the four quarter days which in Gaelic were known as Imbolc, 1 February; Beltane 1 May; Lughnasad, 1 August; and Samhain, 1 November. That these dates have a vast amount of folklore attached to them concerning both the supernatural and observable phenomena is undeniable, but again there is a practicality underlying them which reflects the basic socio-economic structure of society over millennia. Imbolc was the time when the first lambs were born, providing milk and thus butter and cheese after the sterile months of winter. This can be seen in the name itself, *Im* being Gaelic for butter. Beltane has in recent times become the focus of considerable revivals in Scotland and elsewhere, and much of its significance can be seen in the second half of the name, which derives from the Gaelic, *teinne*, meaning fire. Despite a tendency towards a romanticised mysticism in much neo-pagan revivalism, there was always a significant practical aspect to Beltane. Particularly in old traditions from among the Celtic-speaking peoples of the British Isles, Beltane was seen as a time for new beginnings and has been described as a form of New Year.

This we suggest is based on practical, agricultural practice. Enough descriptions of late social and ritual activities at Beltane have survived to let us know that at this time the cattle were driven between two fires and that one of the main constituent woods of these fires was juniper. The smoke of juniper is a well-attested antiseptic; it was used in British Army hospitals as late as the Crimean War and it seems that this may well have been a cleansing of the livestock from ticks and other parasites prior to them being moved away from the clachans and fermtouns. In the Highlands, they were taken to the high pastures and in the Lowlands off into the forest, a term that originally meant no more than uncultivated land. That term is itself somewhat misleading: although much archaeology has focused on the development of fixed field farming, for much of the past seven millennia in Scotland, only the ground immediately around the small communities was intensely farmed.

The wider landscape people had access to, however, was farmed in a different way. A range of berries,

THE CLAVA NE PASSAGE CAIRN, INVERNESS
NH 75759 44470 LAT. 57° 28' 24" N LONG. 04° 04' 24" W

fruits, plants with pharmacological properties, building materials and of course access to both hunting and fishing provided them with a range of other necessities. Remembering that the continuity of occupation of many of these locals lasted for millennia, we can assume that the inhabitants had knowledge of how to utilise their environment with a level of sophistication that is hard for us to imagine, built up over generation after generation. We should also remember that the knowledge of such resources had come down from a period when the entire population were hunter-gatherers.

Lughansad, (1 August) has been interpreted as containing the name of a god-like being, Lugh, who some commentators have interpreted as an actual sun-god. This comes from 12th century Irish literary sources and some caution must be exercised in comparing early Scotland and Ireland in the light of the work of Ewan Campbell, who demonstrates that the Scots of Dalriada, the original Gaelic-speaking part of Scotland, did not in fact come into Argyll from Ulster as settlers or invaders but appear in fact to be every bit as indigenous as the Picts (Campbell: 2001). However, the links and cultural contact between Scotland and Ireland, probably dating from or shortly after the arrival of the first post-Ice Age settlers, strongly suggest a shared cosmological world view. One particular reference, dating from the 16th century, clearly supports this. John Carswell, Bishop of the Isles, who was born at Carnassarie Castle in the Kilmartin Glen, wrote in 1567:

> Great is the blindness and darkness of sin and ignorance and of understanding among composers and writers and supporters of the Gaelic in that they prefer and practise the framing of vain, hurtful, lying earthly stories about the Tuatha dé Danann and about the sons of the Milesius and about the

heroes and Fionn MacCumhail and his giants and about many others whom I shall not number or tell of here in detail, in order to maintain and advance these, with a view to obtaining for themselves passing worldly gain, rather than to write and compose and support that faithful words of God and the perfect way of the truth. (Ross 1976: 17)

What this basically says is that they would rather listen to fairy stories than read the Bible. It also strongly suggests that these stories were well known throughout Scotland and even Carswell knew them. We suggest that this is hardly surprising considering that the Kilmartin is littered with Bronze Age monuments. Such stories could only have come from the local oral culture and not from the Book of Invasions, of which no examples are known in Scotland and the general population could not have bought or even read such an expensive book. We would suggest that such stories, linked to the great variety of ancient monuments in the landscape of Carswell's parishioners, were part of the inherited cultural reverence for the ancestors and suggest that such stories were part of the continuity of commonly held Bronze Age beliefs in Ireland and Scotland and throughout the rest of Europe.

Just as the styles of monuments changed, so stories also altered over time due to cultural change – one particular Scottish example would be the renaming of Wallace's Caves as Prince Charlie's caves after 1745 – but their relationship with the concept of the ancestors and their locales in the landscape were constant. In indigenous lore, a remarkable story links one of our most complex megalithic sites directly to the figure of Lugh from the Tuatha dé Danann. This is at Calanais, where a local tale says that the Shining One walked the central avenue of stones at Midsummer (Swire 1996: 24). It is possible that this may be a reference to rituals performed within the oval shaped circle which is aligned to the midsummer sunrise. Lughnasad itself was an important day that appears to be a celebration of the beginning of the harvest, a time of extremely busy activity but also a celebration of the growth of sustenance for another year.

Samhain has survived in various forms into the modern world as Halloween. At this time it was believed that the barriers between the land of the living and the land of the ancestors, the dead, was penetrable. It is also practically the time for preparing for winter and, just as Beltane was the time to send off livestock to be fattened, this was the time for the slaughter of those beasts not needed to be kept as breeding stock, salting and smoking to preserve them through the winter months. These quarter days can thus be seen as reflecting the necessary realities of a self-sufficient economy, but it could not have escaped our ancestors' notice that each of these feast-days fell almost exactly between an equinox and a solstice.

As discussed earlier, the ancient year seems to have been divided by these significant dates into eight periods of 45 days and each of these dates is utilised in the alignments of ancient monuments. This has been found in Dougie's surveys of Clava and Orkney-Cromarty passage cairns and other monuments such as the Edderton stone circle and its outlying standing stone, which is also carved with a later Pictish, solar double-disc symbol. It is proposed that these monuments were marking sacred times at the eight divisions of the year of a calendar that had already been established long before any of the monuments were built. It is fundamental to human understanding of the world that the sun's light is of great significance – it is as necessary for life as water and this fundamental reality underpins many belief systems around the world. And it is something that did not just last throughout the prehistoric period.

With the advent of Christianity in what are now British Isles, the old ways undoubtedly changed. However, the policy of taking over 'pagan precincts' for new church sites (Bede: 86) meant that the power of the sun, as revered in the monuments and their sites, continued to be central. This is from the Confession of St Patrick: 'the worship of the sun which rises by the command of God, to the worship of the true sun which is Christ, the first leading to pain and damnation, the other to eternal life' (MacCana: 32). There has long been a theory that early Christianity evolved from Roman Mithraism, which was itself linked to the Roman god Sol. The construction of Christian cathedrals and churches has often involved aligning their entrances to the rising sun in the east.

One of the more dominant religious cults in the latter days of the Roman Empire was that of Sol Invictus, the 'Unconquered Sun' and it is widely accepted that the expansion of the Christian Church closely followed the organisational structures of the

Roman Empire itself. The research concluded that there was continuous use of Neolithic and Bronze Age solar spirals throughout the Iron Age and into the early medieval period. This is exemplified by the Chariot of the Sun from Trundholm in Denmark, similar images of which appear on later Iceni and Roman coins and with the solar spirals located at the centre of so many Christian crosses in both Scotland and Ireland. Here, the symbology of the sun has leapt over the divide between pre-Christian and Christian times. That there was some level of rapprochement between the pre-Christian and Christian ideas is reinforced by the use of clearly earlier symbolic references on the Pictish Christian cross-slabs throughout Scotland, as typified by the Glamis Manse cross-slab in Angus (McHardy 2012: 103). In this we see the continuity of solar symbology associated with ritual and belief that had lasted since the Neolithic era and had been carried on into Christian and historic times. It is all too easy in our increasingly complicated technological world to think of ourselves as sophisticated and our distant ancestors, whose technology was so limited by our standards, as primitive. Yet the reality would seem that in their relationship with their own environment, they were much more sophisticated than most humans today. Given the technological limitations of the past, the construction of major monuments reflects a detailed knowledge of the environment in ways that we no longer understand. The instance cited earlier of using seaweed to move huge stones does not just reflect the power of folklore to preserve ancient knowledge, it also shows how the megalith builders interacted with their own environment.

While the practicalities of the calendar were necessary for the pastoral economy of our ancestors, evidence from elsewhere shows that the calendar was something that the first settlers brought with them and in the observance of the eight divisions of the year we see a symbiotic link between the ancestors, the sun and moon, and with the building of the monuments in the landscape, and with the fertility of the earth.

Myth and Remembrance

It is often thought that the past and how we perceive it through history and archaeology is static. In fact, our understanding of how our ancestors lived their time on this fragile planet is always changing.

Compare the crude and clumsy intrusions into ancient monuments in Victorian times with the increasingly technologically sophisticated investigations of today and this change is strikingly apparent. Nowadays, wherever and whenever possible, non-intrusive techniques like magnetometry, Electrical Resistance Tomography and geochemical surveys are used to precede and at times even replace painstaking physical investigation with trowel and brush. Hand in hand with such increasingly technologically driven approaches is the increasing breadth of information we have access to and now consider relevant.

Pollen analysis can tell us much about the staple foods and other crops of the past. Carbon dating gives us increasingly specific time spans and techniques like view-shedding, bringing our understanding of sites and monuments into greater focus within their particular landscapes. Such additions to the investigative tool-box are accompanied by ever larger databases of information gathered from many sites and periods allowing further interpretation. All of this is in a constant flux of development. However, not everything changes. Many sites and monuments have been static for millennia simply due to the fact that they are covered with earth, or because of their location. Others have been left alone out of remembrance of the respect they were given in previous generations – a respect rooted in what we think of today as folklore. It was an attitude inherited from previous generations. With many such sites, there are specific relationships with the landscapes they inhabit. In this book, much of our focus is on Dougie's decades-long investigation of such relationships – specifically on solar and, to a lesser degree, lunar alignments – and how such alignments can help us identify and define locales which appear to have continued to possess considerable relevance to the communities who built and used them. One reflection of this interaction will recur time and again in these pages. The term folklore is by necessity somewhat broad in its meaning, but it reflects the reality that local communities at times hold on to ideas and beliefs that can be useful in helping us interpret many monuments and locales.

Folklore has been central to much of the research that underpins the ideas in this work and we are both certain of its fundamental relevance. The idea that folklore – local knowledge primarily surviving due to having been passed on through oral transmission – is of little or no relevance to interpretation of the past because it is undated and unsourced, is actually unscientific and flies directly in the face of the evidence.

The work of Jennifer Isaacs (op cit) in Australia, showing the existence of scientifically provable material within aboriginal Dreamtime stories over tens of millennia, is supported by specific discoveries. Stuart has developed the process called Geomythography, which draws as much on folklore and landscape reading as anything else to show that the importance of specific locales to nearby communities in many cases has lasted for millennia and, in places, continues today. Ignoring evidence because it has been denigrated in the past is unhelpful. We contend that folklore in all its manifestations, because it derives from the experience of communities with first-hand knowledge of the locales we investigate, is nothing at all like Chinese whispers, although it must be emphasised that a critical approach to such material, as with all potentially useful information, is necessary. Given such an approach, we hope to show that such material is capable of both maintaining and reflecting communities' involvement with important locales, and that this can be of considerable assistance in helping us better understand the ideas and beliefs that held such communities together.

Otta Swire offers an interesting example of this in *The Outer Hebrides and their Legends*. She was told by a man who lived near Calanais that old people locally held certain families in special respect, esteeming them as 'belonging to the Stones', though quite how or why he did not know (Swire 1966). Another individual told her he could remember that when he was a child people visited the stones secretly, especially at Midsummer and May Day (Ibid: 23). Given the reference to May Day, it may have been that the families referred to were associated with the raising of the neid-fire at Beltane (1 May), perhaps inside the central circle. Neid-fire was raised by friction at this important time of the year after all other fire in the vicinity had been put out and all were re-lit from the flames brought about by this process. The complex ceremonies are described extensively in F. Marian McNeill's *The Silver Bough*, in which she explicitly states:

> By primitive peoples, the sun was regarded as the male principle by which the earth, or female principle, was fertilised, and the Beltane festival may be likened to a wedding ceremony where the bride, the Earth, welcomes her lover, the Sun, through whose embrace she shall produce abundance of corn, cattle and men. (Vol. 2: 56ff)

Swire later tells us that marriages consummated inside the circle were believed to be especially blessed and such an idea finds support in folklore directly handed down to the Skye Shennachie, George MacPherson (MacPherson 2001: 104–5).

This linkage of ancient sites, solar alignments and rituals that are clearly focused on the idea of fertility, underlines the importance of the monuments to the local community. MacPherson tells us such acts were performed with the local community looking on, further stressing the linkage between monument, ritual and community. Everyone lives in their own time, but if you inhabit a society where your time is effectively defined by a culture that both respects the past and has a commitment to the future within a long-established communal environment, the ideas that you deal with are linked to a community that crosses time. While societies in many parts of the world have been described as basing much of their ritual behaviour on 'ancestor worship', another way of comprehending this is to see the veneration accorded to those who had gone before as essentially one of respect. The dominant pattern of land occupation, generally referred to as fermtoun and clachan, appears to have originated by the Bronze Age, if not earlier, and continued in most of the country into the 17th century.

This socio-economic conservatism meant that over millennia the vast majority of communities, both Lowland and Highland, were composed of up to a dozen or so kinship-linked families engaged in forms of communal, subsistence-level, pastoral farming, where staples and vegetables were grown close by the individual houses. At the end of this long period, the kinship arrangements which underpinned these communities and held them together had developed in Highland areas into what is known as the clan system, which, although it had been subject to constant change, still preserved the basic kin-based fundamentals of tribal society. That these tribal communities were descended from those mentioned by the Romans almost 2,000 years ago is clear. Similar patterns had developed into the Border family systems and it seems obvious that this process had likewise evolved in the south-west of Scotland until the centralising incursions of David I in the 13th

ROTHIEMAY RECUMBENT STONE CIRCLE, BANFF. MIDWINTER SUNSET, 1992
NJ 55080 48731 LAT. 57° 31' 35" N LONG. 2° 45' 06" W

century. Such communities constantly re-told tales of people and places that had come down directly to them from their predecessors in the same locale, the process of local storytelling, particularly in pre-literate times, always utilising the immediate environment of the community as its backdrop. It is tempting to think that one of the underlying reasons that so many similar socially conservative societies put such a stress on hospitality was that strangers were always welcome because they brought new and different stories to tell. But the local stories, particularly when attached to places of significance that were in themselves reminiscent of the ancestors, were not just an integral part of the culture of these communities – they were in fact the bedrock of such culture. This is not to say that stories did not ever change, only that the underlying realities that gave them importance were so ingrained over generations of retelling that to fundamentally change them would

have destroyed the stories. The time of the story, even the individuals concerned, might change but the fundamental point of any story is what gives it relevance and that does not change. Stories retain their relevance as long as they are told and the very survival of material regarding sites of ancient sanctity and ritual suggests that they have something to tell us, even today.

Alongside the stories, historical, legendary and mythological, specific knowledge regarding weather, agricultural practice and all the practicalities of existing within the local environment were likewise handed on through oral transmission. The development of specific techniques like rhyme, assonance and alliteration, and perhaps even of poetry itself, are likely to have been brought about by the requirement to remember complicated material. Just as our ancestors lived more fully in their physical environment than we do today, so would their powers of memory have been considerably more powerful than ours – because they had to be. It is also worth considering one other fundamental difference between them and us. Literature is designed to be absorbed individually – story functions within and for the community. Electronic media also functions on an individual level but, without the material we have inherited from the past through originally oral sources, there would be few, if any, stories to tell in any medium.

Stories always survive because they had relevance to both storyteller and audience, generally from within the same community, and are based on human experience rooted in the varieties and vagaries of human nature. This does not seem to have changed much, despite our increasing technological sophistication. Throughout Scotland, as elsewhere, many ancient monuments have become associated with 'fairies', known in Gaelic tradition, as noted before, as the *sith*, which apparently gave rise to the practice of so many mounds (not all of which are man-made) becoming known as *sithean*. This, we suggest, is clear evidence that the basic idea behind the fairies was associated with the concept of the ancestors. In an article on such fairy hills, LaViolette and McIntosh write:

> The rich folklore of Scotland, Ireland and Wales provides numerous examples in which certain hills and mounds were recognised as the underground dwellings of the fairy folk. Traditionally such places were viewed with apprehension and fear yet they also represented gateways to another world. Often this was considered to be a world of art and music, which has led Dr John MacInnes of Edinburgh University's School of Scottish Studies to suggest that the fairy hill is a 'metaphor for the imagination'. Following in this vein we wish to establish the cultural significance of fairy abodes thus recognising them, not merely as biological adaptations which meet conservation needs, but as icons in the cultural landscape. (LaViolette and McIntosh 1997: 3)

This idea of the *sithean* as cultural icons places them firmly in the same context as the monuments we consider in this book, as they were perceived of as gateways to the other world of the ancestors. Throughout Scotland, as elsewhere, many such ancient monuments became associated with 'fairies' and it is worth considering whether the monuments and their links to the people of the past gave rise to

the idea of the fairies themselves. Even a superficial reading of the Canmore database (CANMORE) shows that the terms fairy mound and *sithean* are linked to many actual ancient monuments. One example is the An Sithean barrow in Balnaguard in Perthshire, where a stone axe was found. This, we suggest, is clear evidence that such places were associated with the concept of the ancestors and that this is one of the underpinning realities behind the idea of the Fairy Folk here in Scotland and elsewhere. Ireland, which as the megalithic structures there show, clearly shared much of its culture with Scotland in the Stone Age and after. There in the *Book of Invasions* they have a 12th century literary version of tales that most scholars accept is based on indigenous beliefs. We are well aware that these and other similar stories are unlikely to reflect actual events in Irish history and also that they were written in a Christian style used elsewhere. The reason why the monks would describe the old gods is unclear, but it is possible that this was initially to bolster the claims of powerful clans for the sovereignty of Ireland by forming ancestral links with its original inhabitants in their tombs. This would not have been accepted as valid unless the descriptions of the old gods living in the cairns were already known to the general population.

This is exemplified in the propaganda war between the two sets of beliefs, when St Patrick triumphantly throws out the demon Crom Cruach from his gold covered standing stone. This suggests that the Christians also believed that the pagan gods existed. Such beliefs still existed in the late 19th century, as when the Reverend Mackenzie implored an old crofter to move some cup marked stones from his windows, only to be told that this would incur the wrath of the supernatural beings (Sidhe) living within them (Mackenzie 1899–1900: 330). The belief in the Sidhe, as fertility earth gods survived until the late medieval period in Ireland and Scotland, as shown by the aforementioned letter by Bishop Carswell of the Isles, where he tells us that he would rather his flock read the Bible than listen to the stories of the Tuatha dé Danann. As noted, the process of learning such stories was part of ongoing oral tradition and shows that the stories had survived for thousands of years through the Gaelic oral medium in Ireland and Scotland. One of these stories tells us that the sun god Lugh impregnates an earth goddess inside Newgrange and they stop the sun from moving so that their son, the young Angus Og, could be born in one day. This is clearly a metaphor for the rebirth of the midwinter sun entering Newgrange. Considering that the entrance to Newgrange was buried for thousands of years and only re-found in 1699, and that it was only 50 years ago that midwinter sunlight was seen to enter its burial chamber, this shows that this story is 5,000 years old. Orcadian folklore also tells of how Thorodale circles the Odin Stone on his knees for nine full moons before he can look through the hole in the side of the stone (Marwick 1975–6: 32).

The Odin Stone was destroyed in 1814, but its position and that of a companion stone were found by Colin Richards in the late 1980s. The surveys have shown that, from the centre of Stenness, the northern moon would have set in line with the Odin Stone. This confirms the tradition that Stenness is the Circle of the Moon and that the story of the man circling the stone is at least 4,000 years old. The early Church in Ireland and Scotland appears to have melded at some point with indigenous beliefs and it was not the same as the later authoritarian Church of Rome. This can be seen in the adoption of the Druidic tonsure, where the front of the head was shaven in the manner of the Druids. The 'Celtic' church held Easter on the first Sunday after the first full moon after the spring equinox and this in time led to a confrontation with the Church of Rome at the synod of Whitby in 664 AD. While this event is generally stated to have been about resolving the differences over the tonsure and the dating of Easter, the upshot of it was the amalgamation of the original British Church into the Church of Rome. This broke whatever link there had been between the British Church and its indigenous predecessors. The survival of early literary accounts from Ireland, that at the least echo Christian thinking, is unfortunately not matched in Scotland. But given modern understanding of just how tenacious oral tradition is, the possibility exists that there is more to be learned, both from recorded and as yet unwritten indigenous traditions. Stuart is currently investigating the corpus of material regarding the Cailleach, the Hag of Winter, derived from an original Mother Goddess type figure, which in several tales is linked directly with the significant solar date of Beltane. It is also the case that many place-names referencing the Cailleach and her alter ego, Bride, are in close proximity to ancient monuments. The eminent folklorist Eleanor Hull noted in the 1950s that there are many more place-names and stories regarding the Cailleach in Scotland than Ireland, but there is ample evidence that her relationship with the landscape was understood there too. What folklore has preserved in both countries is a common localised association between the monuments, the ancestors and powerful supernatural figures that appear to have considerable significance in pre-Christian thinking in these islands and elsewhere. What we suggest is clear is that the ongoing use of solar and lunar alignments in the creation of funerary monuments is reflective of ideas pertaining to ancestral society that underpinned ritual behaviour over millennia here in Scotland. Continuities can thus be seen between the Bronze Age and earlier and what are generally referred to as Pictish times in the 1st millennium AD. This continuity is reinforced by the process of oral transmission of stories that originated in the far past, and are themselves reflective of ancient ideas relating to the monuments; and in the monuments themselves, we can begin to trace a message in the landscape if, as yet, indistinctly.

Rock Art

Many years ago, when coming off Struie Hill in Easter Ross after a summer's evening of rock climbing, Dougie came across a large cup marked boulder. Cup marks are small hollows ground into rock surfaces and it is thought that their use had spread to the British Isles and Ireland from north-west Portugal during the Neolithic Period around 5,500 years ago. They are found on boulders, bedrock, standing stones and burial cairns and are sometimes surrounded by rings or joined with grooves forming double discs. Although thousands of cup marks occur throughout Europe, there is little to indicate their function in the beliefs of Neolithic or Bronze Age people. Apart from perhaps representing the sun or moon, the only thing Dougie knew about cup marks was that they had traditionally been used throughout Scotland and Ireland for wishing or praying.

Some of the Struie cup marks were carved in dumb-bell shapes, while others formed rows along the top of the boulder, which suggested that they were perhaps the first of the symbols to be carved. Kneeling on the boulder, Dougie deduced that the person making the cup marks would have been facing north-west toward the setting midsummer sun. He returned on 21

June 1987 and watched from the cup marked stone as the midsummer sun set to the right of the mountain of Ben More Assynt. Although he thought that each cup mark could have marked the sun setting along the horizon each night, he knew that this wasn't convincing evidence.

At this time, Dougie had just surveyed the nearby Edderton stone circle and found that its outlying standing stone indicated the sunset in early November and February. The standing stone has a 3rd–6th century AD Pictish salmon and a large double disc and Z-rod carved on its northern side. With the finding of the solar orientation between the circle and the stone, and the joined cup marks and Pictish Double-Disc being basically the same shape, were the later Pictish Double-Disc derived from the Bronze Age cup marks?

This idea was further enhanced while visiting the Ballochmyle cup marked wall in Ayrshire where he noticed that two of the joined symbols looked like Pictish double discs. Dougie also remembered that Professor Charles Thomas had suggested that Pictish symbols had evolved from Bronze Age cup and ring marks (Thomas 1963: 31–97). Surveys over the years of about 100 cup marked monuments found they were generally aligned to the major and minor standstill moon and the sun at the eight divisions of the year. For the sun these were near the winter and summer solstices, the winter and summer quarter days and the equinoxes. On the Aberdeenshire recumbent circles, the cup marks are usually carved on the flankers or the recumbent stone, while at the Clava Cairns near Inverness, they are on the circle and kerbstones or within the burial chambers and passages.

From the centre of the Tordarroch ring cairn, a fallen cup marked kerbstone is directly in line with the highest circle stone and the setting moon near its southern major standstill. On the outer face of the next kerbstone to the west there is a large cup and ring mark, which aligns with the midwinter sunset. At the Gask Clava ring cairn, the midwinter sunset-aligned standing stone is in line with a cup marked kerbstone.

The passage cairn of Newgrange in Ireland also has a number of cup and ring marks along the top of the lintel supporting the roof box, through which the midwinter sun shines into the cairn. Among the cup and ring markings are a spiral and a cup mark with radial lines that looks just like a child's drawing of the sun (O'Kelly 1984: 182). Even though these symbols are hidden, their position suggests they had a religious

STRUIE CUP MARKED STONE, EASTER ROSS

significance to the builders. Below Newgrange, next to the River Boyne, there are two standing stones; from the cup marked north-east stone, the other to the south-west points towards the midwinter sunset. In the opposite direction, every 19–20 years, the stones indicate the northern rising major standstill full moon shortly after the midwinter sun has set.

At Cauldside Burn in Galloway, there is a large boulder carved with cup marks joined by a double spiral which is aligned to the rising and setting midsummer and midwinter sun. From the boulder, five other monuments are aligned to the midwinter sun rising above the hill of Cairnharrow. At Eagerness, also in Galloway, there is a sloping area of bedrock carved with spirals, above which the sun will rise at midwinter. Other cup marked monuments throughout Scotland are aligned to the sun and moon at different times. The double spiral on the southern Temple Wood stone circle near Kilmartin is thought to represent the sun's path across the sky through the year (Scott, J. 1989). The survey from the nearby northern circle showed that the midwinter sun will set in line with that to the south. From cup marks found near the ruined Cill Tobar Lasrach chapel on Islay, the Port Ellen standing stone marked the southern major standstill moon rise. The stone above the Newgrange light box has a frieze of saltire crosses carved along its front and similar symbols can be seen on a sill stone inside the midwinter sunrise aligned passage of Gavrinis in Brittany. From their positions, these saltires could have represented the continuous path of the sun over the years from midwinter to midsummer.

THE STRUIE CUP MARKED STONE
NH 652849, LAT. 57° 50' 2.12" N. LONG. 4° 16' 18" W

Although the setting midsummer sun was first watched from the Struie cup marked stone on 21 June 1987, the above photograph was taken on 19 June 2018.

Circular cross 'Sun Discs' are common on rock carvings in Scandinavia, where they are also associated with the solar ships carrying the dead to the underworld. From the centre of the Stenness stone circle on Orkney, the northern major standstill moon will set behind the stone forming the north-west entrance, which has a cup mark on its lower inner side.

From the nearby Dolmen stones, the northern moon would have also set in line with the holed Odin and its companion stone. In 1703, Martin Martin wrote that 'several Orcadian inhabitants say that Stenness was called the Circle of the Moon and the Ring of Brodgar the Circle of the Sun' (Martin 1703: 365). Young couples about to marry would visit the Circle of the Moon, where the man on bended knee would pledge himself to the woman, after which they would go to the Circle of the Sun, where the woman would pledge herself to the man in the same manner (Marwick in Ritchie 1975–6: 32). The names of these circles could not have been influenced by Stukeley's account of seeing the midsummer sunrise at Stonehenge in 1723, as he published this in 1740, 37 years after Martin. This therefore suggests that these Orcadian traditions were handed down through the generations since the Stenness and Brodgar stone circles were built. Could the solar/lunar aligned cup marked sites imply that most of the other cup marked sites, where an obvious orientation could not be determined, had been used for a similar purpose? The radial groove of the cup and ring marks in the Kilmartin area tended to be orientated towards the north-west and some of those at Cairnbaan and Achnabreck are aligned to the midsummer sunset. Those on the Poltalloch, Kilmichael Glassary and Torblaran outcrops were also aligned to

THE BALLYMEANOCH STONES, KILMARTIN, ARGYLL

The four Ballymeanoch stones are generally aligned to the midwinter sunrise, as shown at about 9.15am on 21 December 2001.

the midsummer and midwinter sun.

At Cloanlawers above Loch Tay in Perthshire, a large natural standing stone marks the rising and setting midsummer sun and the northern major standstill full moon from a number of cup and ring marked boulders. The Ballymeanoch stones near Kilmartin are aligned to the rising midwinter sun and the northern and southern moon during its major standstill. The cup marks on these stones could have reflected rituals carried out at these times. This would explain why the two inside stones are cup marked on opposite sides from each other. Using a right-hand bias, you simply face the carved side of each stone in turn in order to perform the 'ritual', first towards the setting midwinter full moon and then towards the midwinter sunrise. When the sun and moon are in these positions, they are said to be in opposition to each other. This event is symbolised in modern astronomy as a double disc with a connecting rod symbol. This is similar in style to the Bronze Age and Pictish double disc symbols. As the stones are graded in height towards the midwinter sunrise, and in the opposite direction to the setting major standstill full moon, could these symbols represent the sun and moon at this time? While there is undoubtedly a connection with the sun and moon, we are no further forward in knowing what this meant. Initially, the surveys seemed to confirm that the linear settings of cup marks were recordings of solar / lunar events; however, as most of the evidence comes from burial cairns, perhaps they are linked in some way with the ancestors? Some cup marked stones were once part of earlier monuments and were re-used in burial cairns or prised from bedrock to use as standing stones. Perhaps this use of 'old power' legitimised or sanctified the new structures and their continuous use could have formed a deep spiritual connection with the sun / moon and the ancestors. Where the carvings are hidden, they could have functioned like those on

NEWGRANGE PASSAGE TOMB, BOYNE VALLEY, IRELAND
LAT. 53°41'40.90" N LONG. 6°28'32.13"W

The spiral carved kerbstone at Newgrange lies in front of the passage leading into the cairn. Just above this is a special opening called the light box, through which the rising midwinter sun shines into the heart of the burial chamber. The stone above the light box has a frieze of saltire crosses carved along its front, and similar symbols are on a sill stone inside the midwinter sunrise aligned passage of Gavrinis in Brittany. These crosses have also been found on the Ness of Brodgar Neolithic temples on Orkney, and they possibly symbolise the sun.

the inside of burial cists for the exclusive use of the dead, with those on the outside for use by the living. It is likely that rock art had deep religious meanings connected to the ancestors. This can perhaps be seen where cup marked stones were placed in line with the sun and moon on the Bronze Age Clava Cairns near Inverness, or the Nether Largie and Ballymeanoch standing stones in the Kilmartin Glen in Argyll (Scott D 2016). It is accepted that some of the stones of the latter monuments were perhaps cut from carved areas of bedrock. This means that cup marks were still regarded as sacred, and perhaps those in the north-east of Scotland were originally used to hold the 500 or so Neolithic stone balls found is this area? Some of these stone balls are carved with bosses, but 14, such as the Towie ball, have spirals, which link them with those on the midwinter aligned passage tomb of Newgrange in Ireland. Most of these stone balls were found by chance, but one was found within 100 metres of the midsummer sunrise aligned cup marked stone row on Sheriffmuir. Another stone ball was also recently found in the same area. A stone ball and a cup marked stone were found in Structure 10 at the Ness of Brodgar, and they could have been used in the suggested way as the equinox sunlight shone in through its eastern entrance. Perhaps these 'Sun' balls were the original stones placed and turned within cup marks to contact the spirit ancestors as the sun left or entered the Underworld?

Touching the Ancestor Earth Gods

It might seem impossible that such cup mark traditions could have survived for four millennia, yet as they were still being used to the present day, could their traditional use of Gaelic for praying give some insight into their original use? In Scotland and Ireland, to assist childbirth, promote health and ensure fertility in crops and cattle, round stones were turned in cup marks three times *desail* (clockwise) with the sun. This was done in Ireland while praying to St Brigit, known in pre-Christian times as the fertility goddess Bride, whose festival was on 1 February. It was also possible to curse someone by turning the stone three times in an anti-clockwise direction. Similar rituals with cup marks are described by the Gaelic folklorist Alexander Carmichael:

> In many parts of the Highlands... the stone into which women poured the libation of milk is called 'Leac na Gruagach', 'Flag Stone of the Gruagach'. The Fairy Queen who watches over the cows is called the Gruagach in the Islands and she is often seen. In pouring libations to her and her Fairies, various kinds of stones, usually with hollows in them, are used. (Evans-Wentz 1911: 519 n32)

It was believed that if the libation was omitted in the evening, the best cow would be found dead in the morning. There are Gruagach stones on the islands of St Kilda, Skye and Tiree, and she is mentioned in *The Book of Arran*. Near Laggan in Strathspey, offerings of milk or cheese were still being left at a cup mark stone called the 'Clach na Gruagach' in the 1960s, in order to thank the spirits for the protection of cattle and crops, (Richardson 1990: 40). At Tullochgorm Farm in Strathspey, the farmer, Mr Miller, told Dougie that the two standing stones down near the river were 'Pictish elves' known as Mankie and Prunie. These elves were believed to haunt the area around the stones and were always looking for food. In Gaelic, these supernatural spirits are called the Sidhe (*Shee*) and were believed to live in burial cairns and in standing stones. On Orkney, bread or cheese was left at the holed Odin Stone, which was destroyed in 1814 by a southern farmer. This angered the local people who had traditionally used the Odin Stone for making sacred oaths and marriage vows while holding hands through its hole (Ritchie 1975-6: 32). The Odin Stone's former socket and that of another stone were found during excavations in the late 1980s (Richards 1991). Later surveys showed that the two stones once indicated the northern setting major standstill moon and the rising midwinter sun (Scott, D. 2016).

Spirits called the Hogboon are said to live in Orkney cairns and the traditional way of keeping them happy was by pouring milk or beer on top of the mound. Martin describes the same rituals in the Outer Hebrides, to appease a Brownie spirit living within a stone (Martin 1703: 110). In the Norse sagas the elves are similar to the Gaelic Sidhe and they are directly connected with Freyr, the sun god, the fertility of the earth and the Earth Mother. Freyr was said to have been laid in a mound and had offerings made to him. In Sweden, milk was still poured into cup marks in the 1960s to appease the elves (Davidson 1964: 154-6). This custom continued in parts of Ireland and Scotland until the 1960s. Once the food was left for the Sidhe, it was never touched or eaten as it was believed to have no substance. In the Gaelic myths, people visiting the other world of Tír na nÓg are cautioned not to eat any food as they would become one with the dead. This is similar to the Greek myth of Persephone, who can only return to the Earth if she has not eaten while in Hades. This offering of food or libations to the Gruagach and other supernatural beings in return for a supply of milk and crops is the same as the Tuatha dé Danann demands from the Gaels in order to ensure the fertility of the earth. The commonality of these traditions from Sweden to Brittany suggest they are the remnants of Bronze Age beliefs that once existed throughout Europe. In 1899, the Reverend JB McKenzie described how an old crofter some 30 years before would not bury cup marked stones, which were known as 'Clachain Aoraidh' (worship stones), as this would incur the wrath of the spiritual beings living within them (McKenzie 1899-1900). We can now see from other folklore researchers that the use of cup marks was commonly known by the Gaels and that these beliefs had been around for thousands of years long before their 'discovery' in the 19th century. It's unlikely the Victorian rock art researchers would have been given any credit to their indigenous use, as they were the elite of an arrogant empire, engaged in the destruction of what they saw as an inferior Gaelic culture.

Researchers such as Evans-Wentz, Frazer and Gaelic speakers like Carmichael did record these folk traditions but, with rational archaeology being used to understand the past, these beliefs were ignored. These Gaelic traditions seem to suggest that the Fairy Queen and the Gruagach were contemporary expressions of an ancient fertility goddess. In the Introduction to *The Fairy Faith in Celtic Countries,* Carmichael commented:

> The belief in fairies was once common throughout Scotland. It is now much less prevalent even in the Highlands and Islands where such beliefs linger longer than they do in the Lowlands. But it still lives among the old people and is privately entertained even among younger people, some of whom hold the belief, declaring that they themselves have seen fairies.
> (Evans-Wentz 1911)

The Sidhe were called 'The Good Folk' for it was believed that if anyone spoke ill of them, they would destroy their crops and cattle. In the *Táin Bó Cúailnge* (The Cattle Raid of Coolly) the semi-divine hero Cú Chulainn – who was fathered by Lugh, the sun god and was born in Newgrange – falls into an enchanted sleep while sitting against a standing stone. As he dreams, two Sidhe women appear and they tell him that he must visit the otherworld of Tír na nÓg to kill the three sons of Nechtan. To reach the otherworld, Cú Chulainn again falls asleep against a standing stone, which, like burial cairns, are portals to the spirit world. He also impales the daughter and fool of King Ailill on standing stones, which were thereafter called the Finnabair and the Fools stones. There are a number of fool, 'Gowk' or 'cuckoo' stones in Scotland. It is significant that when Cú Chulainn's death occurs at Samhain, his last act is to tie himself to a standing stone. His death at what was the most sacred time for the Gaels would have symbolised the beginning of winter and the death of the sun. It was believed that when the rightful Irish king stood on the Lia Fáil (the stone of destiny) the demon within it would scream out (Dunne 1914). On the same theme, St Patrick drove out and destroyed the demon, Crom Cruach, who lived in a gold-covered standing stone. To the Christians, these spirits were demons. But to people steeped in their ancient myths, this touching of stones would have been seen as connecting to the Sidhe within the stone, which was also a portal to the Otherworld. Professor Charles Thomas has suggested that the spirit of a person becomes one with the stone and he exemplifies this when, in the mountains of central France, he asks a shepherd what a nearby standing stone was for. After he was told that it was 'the giant's stone', Thomas asked, 'Do you mean that the giant was buried under the stone?' 'No!' the shepherd replied. 'He [the giant] was in the stone.' This could explain anthropomorphic-shaped standing stones on the island of Corsica and northern France, and there are also examples of this in Scotland in the Pictish images of the Rhynie man in Aberdeenshire and the warrior on the Collessie stone in Fife. Evans-Wentz refers to such beliefs in *The Fairy Faith in Celtic Countries*:

> Very much first class evidence suggests that the menher, 'standing stone', was regarded by the primitive Celts as an abode of a god or as a seat of a divine power and as a phallic symbol.
> (Evans-Wentz 1911)

At the entrance of the Alley of Dampsmesnil in Normandy is a large female genitalia symbol, known locally as the 'Fertility Goddess'. Among the finds from the excavation of the Alley were human remains, along with polished stone axes, stone arrowheads and animal teeth. Dougie got in touch with Arlette and Alain Cauderlier at the Giverny museum after seeing in one of their website pictures how the low-angled winter sunlight partially entered the Alley. Arlette and Alain then visited the Alley ten days after the winter solstice and photographed the sun setting to the right side of the entrance. Gavrinis in Brittany is also aligned to the midwinter sun, while similar orientations of passage cairns are common throughout Europe. Burial cairns could have been raised to commemorate the collective dead of the community, who in time became revered as the ancestor fertility gods. Powerful individuals in the Bronze Age may have been venerated in this manner up to the early medieval period. The 9th century king of Norway, Olaf, Elf of Geirstad, was sacrificed to in time of famine as, according to tradition, was done to Freyr, god of fertility and fruitfulness (Davidson 1964: 155). The burial mound in Norse mythology is sometimes compared to a house and this might explain the wooden structures found under Bronze Age monuments. A view of the dead in their mounds can be seen in Njáls saga:

It seems to them that the mound was open, and that Gunner had turned himself in the howe and looked up at the moon. They thought that they saw four lights burning in the howe, but no shadow anywhere. They saw that Gunner was merry, with a joyful face.

The alignments of the Carnac stones were also believed to have once been people who turned to stone because they offended the fairies. Surveys of these stones show that they are aligned to the sun at midwinter and to the winter and summer quarter times. There are also Irish stories of Druids turning each other into stones. When Wentz was recording fairy belief on the island of Barra, as he crossed the hills of Beul a' Bhealaich from upper Borve to Sgalary, he stopped by a large stone that he'd been told was haunted by fairies 'which has a key hole in it, for it contains an entrance to a fairy palace' (Wentz 1911: 108). Professor Thom told Dougie that there is a fallen standing stone in this position, but did not mention the 'keyhole', which is possibly a grooved cup and ring mark. The Brevig standing stone, also on Barra, has a cup mark on its eastern side. Ruggles' survey showed that this and another nearby fallen stone had marked the midsummer sun setting on the northern side of the mountain of Heaval (Ruggles 2000: 108. u159. Brevig: 119–20). In the opposite direction, the stones had indicated the sun rising out of the sea in early November and February.

On the hill above Achterneed in Strathpeffer, there is a rock outcrop covered in cup and ring marks. Dougie asked the landowner, Kenny Stewart, if the stone had a name or any traditions and he was told, 'As children, we called it the fairy stone'. Dougie once asked Duncan Williamson, a storyteller of the people known in Scotland as 'Travellers', if he knew what cup marks were used for. At first he was puzzled. But after asking Dougie to describe them, his face lit up and he said, 'They were the Clachan Aoraidh, the worship stones, and by turning a stone within them deiseil, or clockwise with the sun, your wish would be granted.' In order to curse someone, the stones were turned in the cup marks anti-clockwise against the sun. Folklorist Hamish Henderson said that the Travellers had a vast amount of ancient stories and songs that were generally unknown. These traditions were common knowledge to Duncan and many other people living in the Highlands. The idea of spirits living in stones is not limited to the Gaelic areas of Britain; it can also be found other cultures throughout the world. This turning of stones in cup marks is similar to that of the Inuit shamans who used to grind circles into rocks to help them to enter trances so that they could swim through the Earth to the underworld to connect with the spirits of the sun or moon and their ancestors (Freuchen 1961: 213 and Dasent 1900: 149).

There was a traditional medieval belief that some of the circles and standing stones had been people who were turned to stone for dancing on the Sabbath. There are also accounts of stones being able to move and drink from rivers at certain times of the year. It's only now through our ability to gather these traditions from obscure books from the internet that we can see the similarities in these stories which, like the solar aligned monuments, are found throughout north-west Europe and as far south as Morocco. Aubrey Burl has speculated that the broad and narrow stones in the Avebury Avenue could represent the male and female form (Burl 2000: 73 and Evans-Wentz 1911: 108). Similar shaped pairs of solar/lunar aligned stones are found in Perthshire. Apart from the Odin stone, there are other examples where these 'gods' are named. On Colonsay, a survey of two standing stones called Fingal's Limpet Hammers showed that they are aligned on the rising midwinter sun, while Diarmid's Stone at Strontoiller near Oban can be seen in turn from a nearby stone circle and a small kerb cairn to mark the midwinter sunrise and the sunset in early May and August. In Caithness, Lugh's Stone shares the same name as the Irish sun god and it and a nearby standing stone mark the midsummer sunset.

While the names are different, the same theme of supernatural beings associated with or inside stones or cairns occurs time and again. To our modern thinking, these are just fairy stories, but we should remember that billions of people today still have beliefs in other worlds filled with gods, spirits, devils and angels. Of course, we can ignore the folklore and view the past through our modern archaeological and astronomical interpretations. But surely the purpose of archaeology is to rationally assess all aspects of ancient cultures to help us understand their beliefs. It is therefore proposed that the belief of the Sidhe was a diffused cultural memory of the prehistoric ancestors. It would seem that cup marks were where people made contact or left food or gifts on sacred holy days, to ask these powerful gods of the earth to bless the land with fertility and abundance as the sun and moon rose out of and set into the underworld of the dead.

PART 2
Surveys
Douglas Scott

DOUGIE SCOTT SURVEYING

Orkney

STENNESS STONE CIRCLE, ORKNEY

MAPS SHOWING THE MONUMENTS IN THE NESS OF BRODGAR AND STENNESS AREA, ORKNEY ISLANDS

These maps give the location and orientation of the outlying monuments around Stenness. The lochs of Harray and Stenness used to be separated by a thin strip of land in the Neolithic period 5,500 years ago, but they are now joined due to the rise in the sea levels since the end of the last Ice Age.

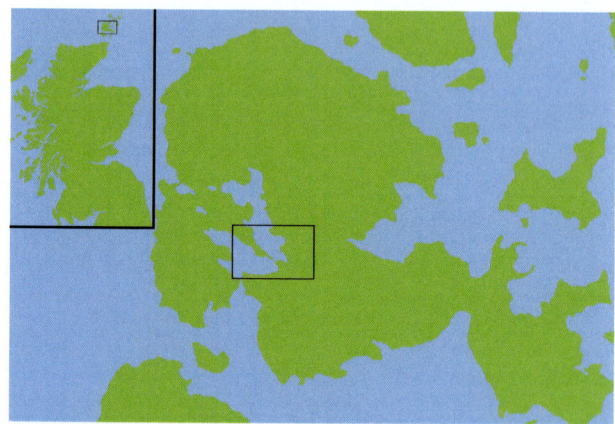

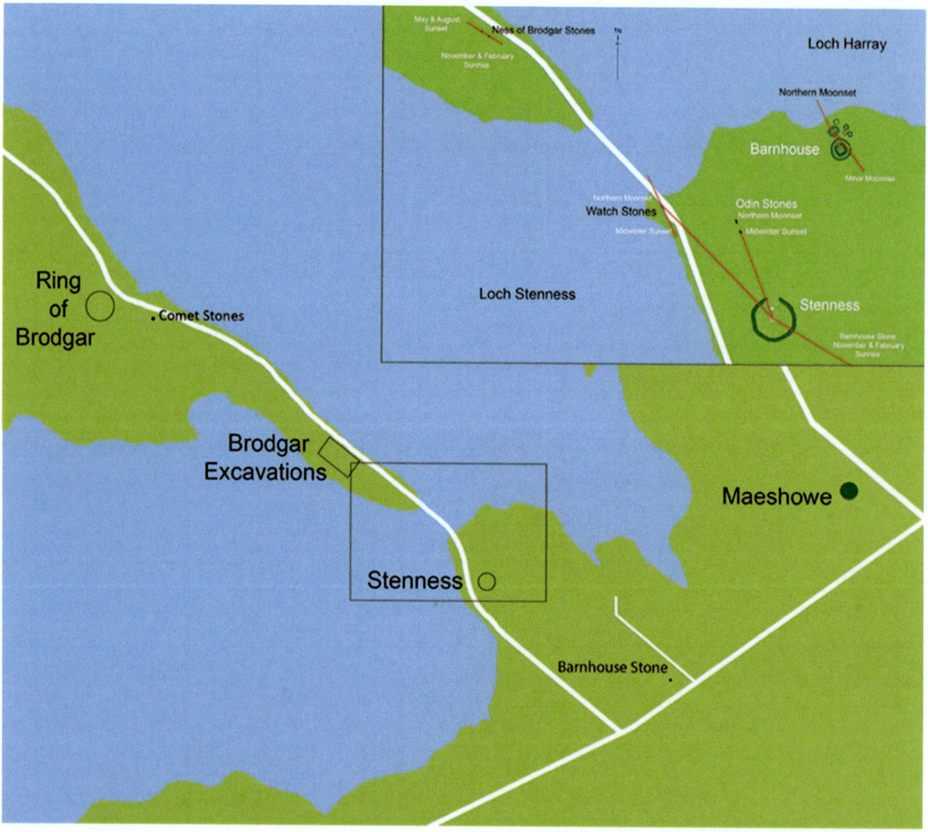

AERIAL VIEW OF STENNESS
HY 30670 12521 Lat. 58° 59' 39" N Long. 3° 12' 30" W

This aerial picture of Stenness shows the central hearth and its remaining stones, with those missing being marked by concrete blocks. The inner rock cut ditch is now filled in and the outer bank is modern. The circle is a slight oval shape and its north to south long axis is generally aligned to the rising southern moon during a major standstill. Colin Richard has shown that the central features found during Ritchie's excavations in the 1970s were the remains of a large squared building that had stood there before the circle was created (Richards 2011: 147–8). Dougie found that the entrance to this earlier building was aligned to the northern setting major standstill moon. A similar shaped and lunar aligned building called Structure 8 was excavated by Richards at Barnhouse, a few hundred metres to the north-east.

Temples of the Sun and Moon

ON THE ORKNEY ISLANDS off the north coast of Scotland, there are some of the most impressive prehistoric monuments in northern Europe. The most famous of these are the Stenness and Brodgar stone circles, the village of Skara Brae and the great burial mound of Maeshowe. Some of these monuments were located on a strip of land that ran between the lochs of Harry and Stenness. People first arrived on Orkney around 8,000 years ago, and they were followed by Neolithic farmers with their new beliefs a few millennia later. The earliest structures on Orkney were built by these Neolithic people 5,500 years ago at Barnhouse near where the Stenness stone circle would be later erected (Richards 2013). The excavation of Stenness found that 12 standing stones had originally stood around a low mound surrounded by a deep rock cut ditch. A central stone hearth was found along with two stone holes and some other features near the circles northern entrance (Ritchie 1975). To the north-west of Stenness, the 3-metre high Watch Stone used to stand in line with another standing stone, the stump of which was found in the 1930s (RCAHMS). The Odin Stone had a hole through it and it used to stand 90 metres to the north-north-west of Stenness, until it was destroyed by a southern farmer in 1814. This incensed the local Orcadians, as they had used it for marriages, or left gifts of food and

THE REMAINS OF STENNESS STONE CIRCLE

The remains of the Stenness stone circle and the locations of the other nearby monuments to the north-west, with the Odin Stones being digitally shown in their approximate positions. From their positions shown in Colin Richards' 1991 excavation report, surveys in 1992 from the central hearth and the Dolmen Stones showed that the northern moon would have set in line with the Odin Stones. The 1992 survey from the central hearth and from the Dolmen Stones showed that the northern midwinter full moon would have set in line with the Odin Stones during a major standstill. The Watch Stone stands next to the road just before the bridge. In 1703, Martin wrote: 'The hills and circles are believed to have been places designed to offer sacrifice in times of pagan idolatry; and for this reason the people call them the ancient temples of the gods.'

pebbles at its base. Children were also passed through the hole to cure them of illnesses. The socket of the Odin Stone and that for another standing stone were found in 1988 (Richards, 1991). In 1703, Stenness and Brodgar were described as the 'Circles of the Sun and Moon' (Martin 1703: 365). Couples wishing to marry would go to Brodgar where the man would kneel and pledge himself to the woman, after which they would go to Stenness where the woman repeated the ritual to the man. The marriage was confirmed when the couple held hands through the hole in the Odin Stone and took the 'Oath of Odin'.

Excavations at the Ness of Brodgar since 2003 have revealed an astounding complex of 5,500-year-old temples that were surrounded by a large stone wall with north-north-west and south-east entrances. Just to the south of the Brodgar temples there are two north-west, south-east aligned standing stones. Some of the rock carvings found on Orkney are similar to those from the burial mound of Newgrange, which, like some Orcadian monuments, is also aligned to the midwinter sun, suggesting cultural links with Ireland. Surveys have shown that the entrances of the Barnhouse buildings were aligned to the midwinter sun and the moon during its major and minor standstills. House 2 was a large squared building and, as a burial cist was found in its entrance passage, it has been described as a cross between a house and a burial cairn (Richards 2013: 82–83). Richards further proposed that the internal features found within Stenness were the remains of a building, similar to Structure 8. Surveys from the central hearths have shown that the entrances of these buildings were aligned to the northern setting major standstill moon.

THE LARGE DOLMEN STONE AT STENNESS, LOOKING TO THE FORMER POSITION OF THE ODIN STONES

Graham Ritchie told Dougie that he thought the large Dolmen stone had originally stood on its west end as a standing stone (Ritchie, *pers. comms*). From the Dolmen Stones near midwinter, the northern major standstill full moon would have set in line with the Odin Stones every 19–20 years, Azi. 336°. Alt. 0° 20'. Decl. +27° 54'. The two smaller standing stones are generally aligned to the northern moon setting near the Odin Stones. To the south-east, they mark the midwinter sunrise 5,000 years ago.

'CIRCLE OF THE MOON'

This digitised picture shows how the northern major standstill midwinter full moon might have looked as it set in line with the Odin Stones. This will occur within a two-week period of the winter solstice. This also confirms Martin's comments that Stenness is the 'Circle of the Moon'.

Orcadian folklore tells how a man called Thorodale would visit the Odin Stone for nine full moons and circle it nine times on his knees, before looking through the hole in its side (Marwick 1975). Given the lunar alignment of the Odin Stones, this would suggest that this story is 5,000 years old and it is describing rituals carried out as the moon set in line with the Odin Stones.

GHOST IMAGES OF THE ODIN STONES
HY 30810 12600 LAT. 58° 59' 42" N LONG. 3° 12' 21" W

Ghost images of the Odin Stones are used to show how they were aligned to where the midwinter sun would have originally risen above Stenness, Azi. 156° Alt. 3° Decl. 24° 30". Due to the shift in the Earth's axis, the midwinter sun now rises on the horizon to the left of the picture. Perhaps the first Viking settlers on Orkney called it the Odin Stone because they associated the hole in the stone with their one-eyed Norse god. Odin sacrificed his eye to drink from the well of wisdom, and perhaps this is why Thorodale circled the stone on his knees, so he could look through the hole in the Odin Stone to define the future. Looking through holed stones is a common theme in Gaelic folklore and such a stone was used for this by the legendary Easter Ross Brahan Seer, Kenneth Mackenzie.

LOCATION OF STONE 6, STENNESS

The excavations of Stenness show where Stone 6 once stood before it and the Odin Stones were destroyed by a southern farmer, who was unaware or did not care that the stones were sacred to the Orcadians. This farmer only halted his destruction of the stones when he was threatened with legal action. A ghost image is used here to show the original position of Stone 6. From the centre of Stenness, the sun set above the Ring of Brodgar at 9.12 pm on the 7 August 2014. This will also occur in early May, and these times were later known as the festivals of Lughnasad and Beltane. The full moon will set in line with Stone 5 near the spring equinox.

LOCATIONS OF STONES 2 AND 3, STENNESS

The surveys in 1992 revealed from the centre of Stenness that each of the stones marked the rising and setting sun and moon at different times. The southern major standstill moon will set behind Stone 2 every 19–20 years and, as shown at 3.45pm on 19 December 2018, the midwinter sun will set in line with Stone 3, and on the southern side of Ward Hill on the island of Hoy.

STENNESS STONE CIRCLE

This picture shows the midsummer sunrise at 4.28am on 27 June 2018, which would have originally risen in line with the destroyed Stone 9.

AERIAL PICTURE OF BARNHOUSE

BARNHOUSE TEMPLES
HY 30672 12515 LAT. 58° 59' 45" N LONG. 3° 12' 24" W

The Barnhouse settlement was found a few hundred metres to the north-east of Stenness by Colin Richards in 1984. The excavations from 1986–91 revealed that the remains of 15 buildings, some of which overlay earlier structures, had been built in the Neolithic Period 5,000 years ago. These buildings had hearths, stone beds and, as the second largest House 2 had a burial cist in its passage, it has been compared to a passage cairn. Groove Ware pottery and flint tools were also found within these buildings which were destroyed in 2600 BC to build a large temple known as Structure 8. The entrances of these buildings were found to be aligned to the rising and setting midwinter sun, and to the moon at its southern and northern minor and major standstills.

Houses 2-3-6 and Structure 8 have been reconstructed and the aerial picture shows the proposed solar or lunar orientations of their entrances. The entrance of Structure 8 is aligned to the setting moon near, but not at its extreme northern major standstill. This is similar to the orientation of the entrance of the large temple that stood at where the Stenness stone circle would be later built. This, along with the finding that other monuments throughout Britain were generally aligned to the sun and moon, supports Dr Euan MacKie's suggestion that these cultures were presided over by some kind of astronomer priests.

THE WATCH STONE, NORTH-WEST OF STENNESS STONE CIRCLE
HY 30548 12639 Lat. 58° 59' 43" N Long. 3° 12' 38" W

The Watch Stone is over 5 metres high and the stump of another stone was found some 5 metres to the south-east during road works in 1936.

WATCH STONE SURVEY

To the north-west, the Watch Stone is aligned to the setting midwinter major standstill full moon, Azi. 334°. Alt. 0° 30'. Decl. +27° 30'. These are approximately the same orientations as the alignments of the Odin Stones.

A survey of the flat side of the Watch Stone suggests that it is likely that both of these stones were aligned towards the rising midwinter sun, Azi. 156°. Alt. 3°. Decl. -24° 30'. It has been suggested that the Odin and Watch Stones were part of a ceremonial avenue linking Stenness with the Ring of Brodgar, but there is no archaeological evidence to support this view.

NESS OF BRODGAR STANDING STONES
HY 303128. LAT. 58° 59' 49" N. LONG. 3° 12' 50" W

THE NESS OF BRODGAR TEMPLES

The sun will set in line with the stones in early May and August, as shown on 7 August 2014. The Ness of Brodgar excavations are on the other side of the house.

The Ness of Brodgar

The two stones shown above stand near the southeast entrance of the wall that once surrounded the Ness of Brodgar complex of 20 or so temples, which have been under excavation since 2005. The wall's path to the right along the lower eastern side of the peninsula is unclear, and it probably lies under the road. The earlier temples were eventually destroyed in order to build a large building nicknamed by the excavators as the 'Cathedral' because of its size. In time, even the 'Cathedral' and wall were razed to the ground and the site was apparently abandoned. The fact that these stones are still standing could mean that they were perhaps erected for ritual activity during the later Bronze Age after the temples were destroyed. Unfortunately, the above house blocks the view to the north-west, but surveys in 1992 suggested the stones indicated the setting sun in early May and August, some 45 days before and after midsummer. Dougie took the above photograph. The general orientation of the strip of land between the two lochs is towards the rising and setting sun in early November, February, May and August.

Perhaps these solar orientations are why the Ness of Brodgar complex was built there. More than 20 years after first surveying these stones, Dougie took a photograph of the sun setting over the house from a high campole on 7 August 2014. This will also occur in early May. From the centre of the Ness of Brodgar complex, the sun will also appear to set into the Ring of Brodgar around these times. Even if the 'Cathedral' was still standing by the time these stones were erected, it would not have obscured the sunset at these times. Some archaeologists have proposed that the Ness stones and the Odin and Watch Stone

THE NESS OF BRODGAR TEMPLES
HY 30282 12876 Lat. 58° 59' 50" N Long. 3° 12' 55" W

The view to the east from Structure 12 towards Maeshowe. The sun will rise above Maeshowe for a few days around the spring and autumn equinoxes on 21 March and 21 September.

alignments were once part of a ceremonial avenue of standing stones linking Stenness with the Ring of Brodgar. There is, however, no archaeological evidence to support this idea, whereas there are numerous examples throughout Europe of rows of standing stones being aligned to the sun or moon.

The excavation of the remains of this complex was instigated when a carved stone was found in 2002. The excavations since then have revolutionised our view of life in the Neolithic period and have revealed that these 5,500-year-old buildings were not lived in and are thought to have been temples. A wonderful array of triangular carvings, plus a stone mace, axe heads and a stone ball have also been found. Some of the temple doorways are cup marked or carved with a 'Butterfly' symbol unique to Orkney and Caithness. This, along with spiral carvings from Eday Manse, suggests a cultural connection with the rock art of the Boyne valley in Ireland. These links were probably maintained with the people of the Calanais stone circles on the Isle of Lewis by sea, or down along the east coast of the Moray Firth via the Great Glen.

Structure 1 is thought to be the first building to be erected on the site, and surveys of the entrances of six of the buildings have shown that they were solar and lunar orientated. Just a few metres from the south-east cup marked entrance of Structure 1, there is the stump of a standing stone, which would have indicated the rising southern major standstill moon. The moonrise would be later hidden by Structure 12 in the background, but the orientation of the standing stone to the moon from within Structure 1 must have been of great significance. Other blocked solar/lunar aligned 'sightlines' also occur at buildings at Barnhouse and at some Clava type passage cairns near Inverness. It is impossible to estimate the height of the wall, but as it stood at a distance from any of these buildings, it is likely it would be well below the level of the south-east horizon.

Eventually, all the other buildings were pulled down in order to construct Structure 10, the largest

THE EQUINOX SUNRISE FROM STRUCTURE 10, 'THE CATHEDRAL'

At 7.16am on 21 September 2016, the partially obscured equinox sun rose just to the north of Maeshowe. The squared shape of the Structure 10 can be made out under the protective plastic sheeting and the stump of the standing stone can be seen to the bottom of the picture.

temple on the highest part of the Ness of Brodgar. Although Structure 10 was built with very thick walls, its interior is small with a central hearth and the remains of a stone dresser near the back west wall. The eastern entrance to the 'Cathedral' is aligned towards the burial mound of Maeshowe, above which the sun will rise at the spring and autumn equinoxes. Such a deliberate orientation would suggest that the wall around the Brodgar temples was also removed. The function of the 500 Neolithic stone balls is unknown, but as 14 are carved with spirals similar to those on Newgrange in Ireland, they perhaps symbolise the sun. Votive offerings of a stone ball, a human bone and that of a bird were placed under the south-west buttress inside Structure 10 at the Ness of Brodgar to prevent it from collapsing. Before this, the highly prized stone ball could have been placed in a cup marked stone found within the 'Cathedral' each time the equinox sunlight flooded into the temple as the sun rose out of the Underworld above Maeshowe. Structure 10 was later destroyed with signs of a great feast of cattle, the bones of which were then spread over the flattened temple.

SALTIRE CROSS SYMBOLS, STROMNESS MUSEUM

Hundreds of pieces of rock art have been found at the Ness of Brodgar and these saltire cross symbols from the 'Cathedral', now in Stromness Museum, are similar to the friezes above the entrance of the midwinter aligned passage cairns of Newgrange in Ireland, and within the passage of Gavrinis and Brittany. Rock carvings of crosses within circles are common throughout Scandinavia but are rare in Britain, with one being carved of the buried Cochno stone in Glasgow. Such crosses are also found on gold sun discs. This symbol is also similar to the symbol used by archaeoastronomers to explain the solstices. Perhaps these cross-shaped 'solar' symbols were placed to 'strengthen' the Cathedral's foundations.

THE RING OF BRODGAR
HY 295134. LAT. 59° 0' 5". N. LONG. 3° 13' 47" W

The Ring of Brodgar

Further along the peninsula to the north-west is the 5,500 years old Ring of Brodgar, originally comprised of 60 stones, of which only 27 remain standing. This 103-metre wide stone circle is the largest in Scotland and it is enclosed within a wide rock cut ditch with two opposite entrances to the north-west and south-east. On the high north-west horizon, the Bookan and Buckan cairns could probably be seen against the sky, and there are also four large burial cairns and some smaller cairns scattered around Brodgar. A short distance to the east is the 2-metre high Comet Stone. The circle stones apparently came from various parts of Orkney, leading to the idea that different island communities were involved in the collective building of the circle. Perhaps this was achieved by the people being motivated by their religious beliefs. It has been speculated that people travelled through Brodgar while visiting the other monuments on the peninsula on some kind of pilgrimage (Richards 1992).

Although the Ring of Brodgar was traditionally called the Circle of the Sun (Martin 1703) there is no definitive evidence that any of its 60 stones were used to indicate the sun. However, from the solar/lunar aligned monuments nearby and the hundreds of others found throughout Scotland, it seems obvious that the builders of Brodgar knew which stones marked the rising and setting sun. Surveys in the early 1990s suggested that some of the mounds around Brodgar were generally aligned to the rising moon during its minor standstill. The northern major standstill moon will rise above the north-east cairn; however, none of the other three large mounds showed any significant solar or lunar orientation. Archaeologist Colin Richards commented that the visibility from

Brodgar of the ruined Staneyhill horned cairn might have had some significance (Richards 2013: 181). From Brodgar and Stenness, the midsummer sun rises above the Staneyhill cairn. There are no obvious traces of a burial chamber or passage, but the long axis of this cairn is aligned towards the midwinter sunrise and the midsummer sunset. From the cairn, the sun will rise in line with a standing stone 385 metres uphill to the south-east in early November and February.

The only possibly external indications to the sun or moon from the centre of Brodgar are the Comet Stones, which also align with Maeshowe. The sun and moon will rise above the Comet stones and Maeshowe at different times some two weeks before and after the spring and autumn equinoxes. The sun will also rise above the Stenness stone circle in early November and February. This direction is commonly found in the Orkney-Cromarty passage cairns (Scott, D. 2016). The Pleiades constellation would also have appeared above Maeshowe 5,500 years ago. This perhaps gives some credence that Orkney was the island of the Hyperboreans mentioned in the writings of Diodorus Silicus, who, in 44 BC, quotes from the

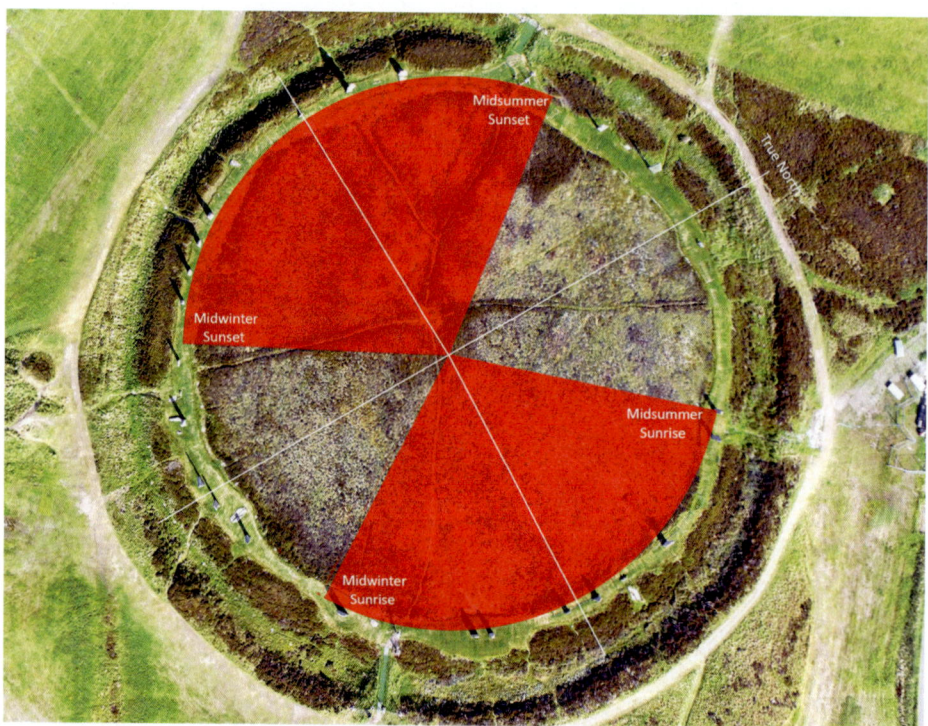

POSITIONS FOR THE RISING AND SETTING SUN FROM THE CENTRE OF THE RING OF BRODGAR

Although there are no obvious solar indications from the centre of Brodgar, given the orientations of the nearby monuments to the sun and moon on Orkney and the rest of north-western Europe, it would be unlikely that it was not used for this purpose. From the Ring of Brodgar, the sun will rise in line with Stenness in early November and February at the times that were later known as the festivals of Samhain and Imbolc. The above aerial picture shows the approximate rising and setting positions for the sun from midsummer to midwinter. Also note how similar this shape is to the symbols found at the Ness of Brodgar.

THE RING OF BRODGAR

From the Ring of Brodgar, the midsummer sun as it rises above the Staneyhill long cairn at 4.21am on 27 June 2018. Waiting in the quiet of the predawn, Dougie imagined Brodgar filled with people who had perhaps travelled from all over Britain to celebrate the midsummer sunrise.

earlier work of the historian Hecataeus, from around 500 BC:

> This island is situated in the north, facing the land of the Celts and is inhabited by the Hyperboreans, who are called by that name because their home is beyond the point where the north wind blows; and the land is both fertile and productive of every crop, and since it has an unusually temperate climate it produces two harvests a year. Moreover, the following legend is told concerning it: Leto (who was the mother of Artemis and Apollo by Zeus) was born on this island, and for that reason Apollo is honoured among them above all other gods: and the inhabitants are looked upon as priests of Apollo, after a manner, since daily they praise this god continuously in song and honour him exceedingly.
>
> And there is also on the island both a magnificent sacred precinct of Apollo and a notable temple, which is adorned with many votive offerings and is spherical in shape. Furthermore, a city is there which is sacred to this god, and the majority of its inhabitants are players on the cithara; and these continually play on this instrument in the temple and sing hymns of praise to the god, glorifying his deeds. The Hyperboreans also have a language, peculiar to them, and are most friendly disposed towards the Greeks, and especially towards the Athenians and the Delians, who have inherited this good will from most ancient times. The myth also relates that certain Greeks visited the Hyperboreans and left behind them costly votive offerings bearing inscriptions in Greek letters. And in the same way Abaris, a Hyperborean, came to Greece in ancient times and renewed the good will and kinship of his people to the Delians. They say that the Moon, as viewed from this island, appears to be but a little distance from the Earth and to have upon it prominences, like those of the Earth, which are visible to the eye.
>
> The account is also given that the god visits the island every 19 years, the period in which the return of the stars to the same place in the heavens is accomplished; for this reason the Greeks call the 19-year period the 'year of Meton'. At the time of this appearance of the god, he both plays on the cithara and dances the night through, from the vernal (spring) equinox until the rising of the Pleiades, expressing in this manner his delight in his successes. The Kings of this city and the supervisors of the sacred precinct are called Boreades, since they are descendants of Boreas and the succession to these positions are always kept in their family.

THE COMET STONES
HY 29631 13321 LAT. 59° 00' 04" N LONG. 3° 13' 36" W

To the east of the Ring of Brodgar, the 2-metre high Comet Stone stands on a low flat-topped mound in a curious right-angled setting with the stumps of two former standing stones. According to Orcadian folklorist George Marwick, the Comet Stone was traditionally called the 'Ulie' or 'Oily Stane' and men, when passing the stone, used to doff their hats as a sign of respect. Perhaps its name reflects a time when oil or butter was poured over the stone as a votive offering.

HIGH VIEW OF THE COMET STONES

The stumps of the two former standing stones are visible, set at right angles to the Comet Stone.

The Comet Stones

Surveys in 1992 showed that the stumps were aligned towards the midsummer sunrise, and in the opposite direction to where the minor standstill moon will set in line with some burial cairns on the nearby south-west horizon. From the Comet Stone, the midsummer sun will set in line with the northern stump and, in the reverse direction, the minor standstill full moon will generally rise in line with the Comet Stone, Azi.138°. Alt. 2°. Decl. -20°. The Comet Stone has nothing to do with comets and the name was derived from a 19th century astronomical idea that it was 'orbiting' the Ring of Brodgar.

THE COMET STONES AND THE RING OF BRODGAR TO THE NORTH-WEST

At 8.45pm on 26 June 2018, the sun was photographed setting in line with the Comet Stone and the stump of the northern stone. Originally the sun would have been hidden behind the northern stone in the weeks leading up to midsummer. However, as shown below with the digital creation of the two former standing stones, the northern stone could have been placed so that the setting sun appeared on its right side at the summer solstice. Azi. 321°. Alt 1°. Decl. +24°.

THE COMET STONES TO THE SOUTH-WEST

The following morning, on returning to the Comet Stones to photograph the midsummer sunrise, Dougie was surprised to see a beautiful red moon appear through the mist, where, as predicted, it set in line with the nearby burial cairns, Azi. 223°. Alt. 2°. Decl. -20°. Originally, the minor standstill moon would seem to have set into the taller cairns in line with the former standing stones, but as it was a little higher, this is why it set to the right of the cairns.

THE COMET STONES TO THE NORTH-EAST

About an hour and a half after the moon had set, the midsummer sun rose in line with the two standing stones stumps at 4.22am on 27 June 2018, Azi. 40° 48'. Alt. 1° 30'. Decl. +23°30'. There is little doubt that the Comet Stones were deliberately set up to mark the rising and setting midsummer sun and the moon during minor standstills. If these stones marked burials, perhaps it was believed that the spirit ancestors were energised by the sun at these times to enhance the fertility of the surrounding fields?

THE BARNHOUSE STONE WITH MAESHOWE TO THE NORTH-EAST
HY 31268 12165 LAT. 58° 59' 28" N LONG. 3° 11' 52" W

From Maeshowe, the Barnhouse Stone generally marks the setting sun near midwinter. From the Barnhouse Stone 5,000 years ago, the summer solstice sun would have risen directly above Maeshowe,
Azi. 42°. Alt. 2°. Decl. +24°.

THE BARNHOUSE STONE WITH MAESHOWE TO THE NORTH-EAST

By the time Dougie got to the Barnhouse Stone at 4.38am on 27 June 2018, the sun had just risen above the higher horizon, which had been hidden by a bank of fast moving cloud. The position of the midsummer sun today is due to the slight change in the Earth's axis over the past 5,000 years. Maeshowe is now hidden from the Barnhouse Stone by a nearby dyke and the picture below was taken from across the field so that the cairn could be seen.

THE MODERN ENTRANCE OF MAESHOWE
HY 31820 12770 LAT. 58° 59' 48" N LONG. 3° 11' 18" W

The midsummer sun rising from behind Maeshowe at 5.02am on 27 June 2018.

Maeshowe

Maeshowe is one of the finest passage cairns in Western Europe and it is placed on an oval platform surrounded by a ditch and bank. The squared central chamber has what might be three small burial chambers built into its 4-metre-high walls, which were covered by a corbelled roof. The four standing stones placed at the corners of the chamber do not support the roof, and these and the large stones of the south-west aligned passage could have come from an earlier stone circle that was demolished to build Maeshowe. Maeshowe's internal structure is a cruciform shape and it is accepted that its passage is aligned to the midwinter sunset.

The 12th century Orkneyinga Saga describes how Vikings led by Earl Harald took shelter in Maeshowe (Meyjarhaugr or Maiden's Mound) during a snowstorm and recounts that two of his men went insane. In 1861, Farrer and Petrie tried to enter Maeshowe by its original lower outer passage, which they said was 22 feet long and 2 feet 4 inches square, but this

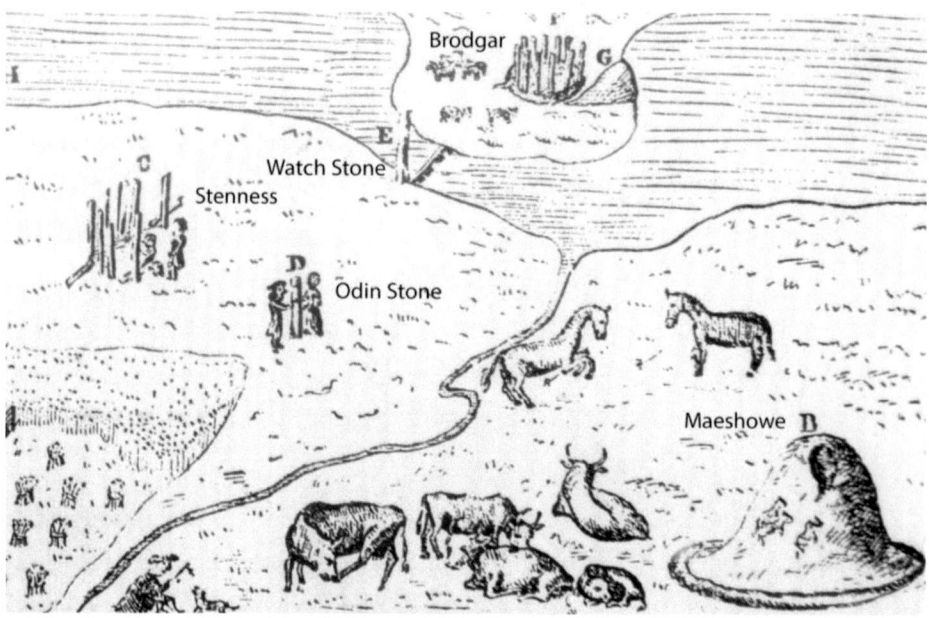

PART OF LOW'S DRAWING OF STENNESS AND BRODGAR

Part of Low's 1772 drawing showing the Stenness and Brodgar stone circles, and the large hole on top of Maeshowe he said was dug by Oliver Cromwell's troops (Anderson 1879). According to the tradition, a kneeling woman at Stenness is pledging herself to her intended husband, and their marriage is sealed when they hold hands through the hole in the Odin Stone. Farrer describes Maeshowe as being 42 feet or 12 metres high, whereas now it is 7 metres high. This means that the 5 metres of earth were removed perhaps when the roof was repaired in the 1860s. An 1862 watercolour painting depicting Maeshowe as a high cone shape truncated by the hole in the roof before it was repaired can be seen in the HES Canmore site.

was blocked with a large pile of earth that had fallen through a hole in the roof of the main chamber. Farrer entered the chamber through this hole and he commented that it had probably been made by the Northmen (Farrer 1861). After clearing out the fallen earth, Norse runes and Neolithic symbols were found carved on the chamber walls. The runes told how Vikings had sheltered in the mound from a blizzard and it had taken three days to remove a vast treasure that they found in Maeshowe. In his 1772 book, the Reverend George Low shows in a drawing a large hole on top of Maeshowe, which he said was made by Oliver Cromwell's troops in the 1660s (Anderson 1879). This means that the Vikings could only have entered Maeshowe along its passage.

Petrie drew the full length of Maeshowe's passage in some simple plans, but in his more accurate drawings its outer part was truncated to fit in Farrer's book. Copies of Petrie's plans by Dryden, Burke and Calder are used here as they show more of the details of the inside of the mound, with Dryden's copy depicting the full length of the passage. There are no detailed public records about what occurred at Maeshowe after its excavation, but it seems that about this time the lower 6.6-metre length of the outer passage was removed, and the modern entrance built. This was perhaps done when the roof was repaired in the late 1860s. Magnus Spence was the first to notice that the midwinter sun light entered Maeshowe's passage in 1893 (Spence 1906). As the

A DIGITISED VIEW OF ORIGINAL SIZE OF MAESHOWE

We are used to how Maeshowe looks today, but based on Farrer and Low's description perhaps this digitised image gives a closer impression to how it and its smaller entrance originally looked. In Orcadian folklore, Maeshowe was inhabited by a Hogboon guardian spirit that looked after the fertility of the land around the cairn. This spirit was kept happy with beer being poured on top of the cairn. Martin describes similar Hebridean rituals of pouring milk on small hills (burial mounds) and large stones, which were believed to be inhabited by Brownie spirits (Martin 1703: 110). In Sweden, these mound dwellers, or draugrs, were thought to be vampires (Davidson 1964: 54). Perhaps the terrifying thought of crawling into a dark haunted tomb is why two of Earl Harald's men went mad.

sun sets on Ward Hill some 28 days before midwinter, this causes its low angled light to touch the back wall of the central chamber, but this only occurs today because the outer passage was removed in the 1860s. By adding the missing section from Dryden's to Calder's plan, this shows the sunlight would only have reached halfway along the passage. By adding the original length and lower height of the outer passage from Dryden's to Calder's plan, we can see that the midwinter sunlight could not have entered the central chamber. Similar to that at Newgrange, it has been proposed that Maeshowe might have had a light slit, through which the midwinter sunlight shone along the passage into the central chamber (Welfare and Fairly 1980: 93). However, Petrie's and Burke's detailed plans clearly show that this area was blocked by the lintel stones of the original low outer passage. It is proposed that the main focus of interest were the three small burial chambers off the central chamber, as they are generally in line with the midwinter sunrise, and the rising and setting midsummer sun.

This information might not be generally accepted as Maeshowe's supposed midwinter alignment is a major draw for many people visiting the monument, but the evidence is now overwhelming. The midwinter sunlight entering Maeshowe was archaeologically accepted because it was part of the cultural link to Newgrange in Ireland. Apart from saying that Farrer entered Maeshowe, there is no mention in the archaeological record of him finding, or trying to enter the monument by its passage, and the focus has since been on its Viking runes and its supposed midwinter alignment. The Neolithic builders of Maeshowe could easily have aligned the passage to where the winter solstice sun set on the lower horizon to the left of Ward Hill, but this would have changed the solar orientations of the three small burial chambers. Although these events could not have been seen from inside the central chamber, they show the sacred connections between the sun and the ancestors. Similar hidden, or symbolic, solar and lunar orientations have also been found in the false portals and axis alignments of some Clava type passage cairns near Inverness (Scott, D. 2016). This can be best seen in the long axis of the egg shaped Druid temple passage cairn, which from within its central burial chamber

was aligned to the hidden midwinter sunrise and the setting northern major standstill moon. Like the hidden orientations within Maeshowe, these were likely focused on the spirit ancestors within the cairns whose veneration could perhaps be compared with that of the later Christian Saints. The photograph of the midsummer sun rising from behind Maeshowe on 27 June 2018 shows how the sun would have originally risen in line with the long axis which runs along the line of the passage.

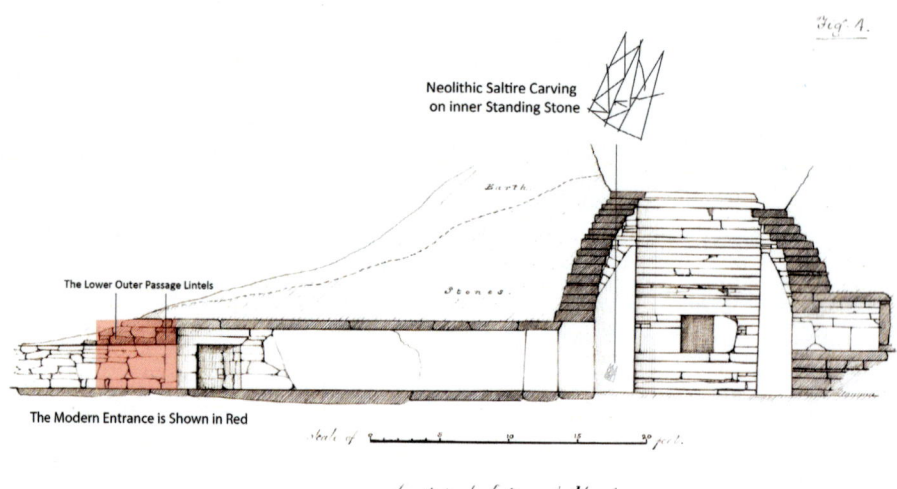

BURKE'S COPY OF PETRIE'S SIDE ELEVATION OF MAESHOWE

Although the full length of the lower outer passage is not shown in Burke's copy of Petrie's plan, as there are lintel stones above its inner area, it is proposed that like Newgrange, it was completely covered to its original entrance. To gain safe access into the central chamber, Ferrer may have enlarged the hole made by Cromwell's troops, and Petrie's plans also show how much of the top of the mound has been removed. Just inside the higher passage on the left, there is the specially built niche that today holds a squared stone which is thought was used to block the inner end of the lower passage. The only place where a light slit could have been built in Maeshowe's passage, is above the modern entrance, which is shown in above in red. Petrie and Burke's detailed plans clearly show that this area was closed by the lintel stones of the original lower outer passage.

Courtesy of HES (Society of Antiquaries Scotland)

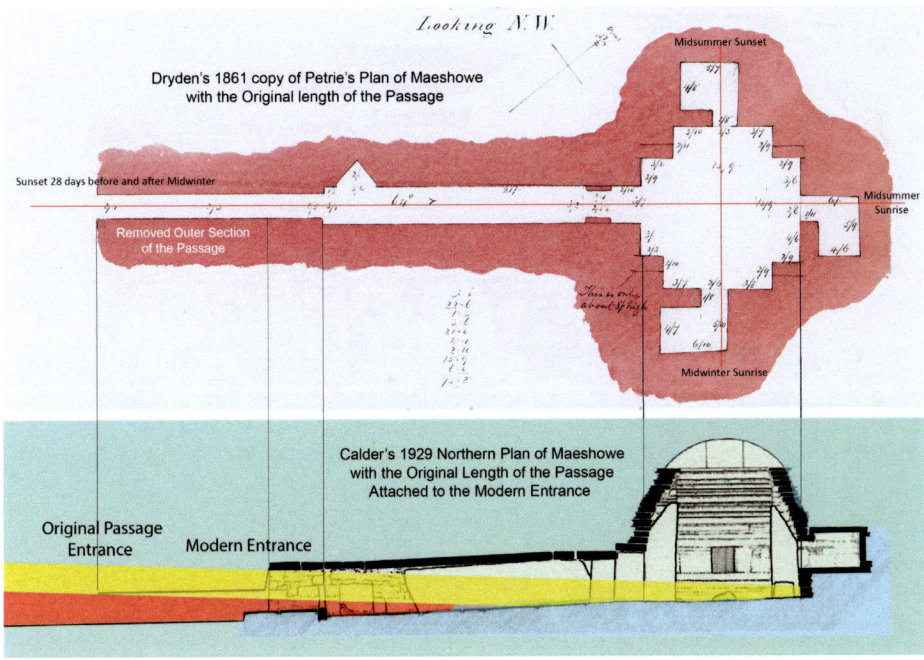

DRYDEN'S AND CALDER'S PLANS OF MAESHOWE

The latest available plans of Maeshowe were drawn by Calder in 1928, 67 years after the outer passage was removed. It also shows that the passage rises towards the central chamber. HES also comments that the present entrance is modern. By adding Dryden's outer passage to Calder's plan, it is possible to show that when the sun originally set on top of Ward Hill some 28 days before midwinter, its light, shown here in red, would only have reached halfway along the passage. The yellow line shows how the midwinter sunlight will enter through the modern entrance today. In the 150 years since Farrer entered Maeshowe, it has unwittingly been reduced to half its original height and the removal of the outer passage now allows the midwinter sunlight to enter the cairn. This was never intended by its builders. However, although this could never have been seen from inside the cairn, surveys show the three small cells were generally orientated to the rising and setting midsummer sun and the midwinter sunrise.

Courtesy of HES (Society of Antiquaries Scotland)

THE ENTRANCE OF MAESHOWE'S PASSAGE

As shown in Petrie's drawing, the low roof of the outer passage would have been covered with roofing slabs, and this has been digitised in white above to show how it might have originally looked. The blocking stone can be seen on the left just inside the higher passage. When this stone was dragged into position, there would have been a small gap between its top and the roof of the lower passage. However, the low angled sunlight could not have reached high enough up the blocking stone to have entered the inner passage. The height of the lintels of the inner passage is shown in Petrie's plans as roughly the same as that of the niche holding the blocking stone. It would have been difficult to move this stone in the narrow confines of the inner passage to get into the central chamber, and just as hard to drag it back to seal the tomb. Patrick Ashmore proposed that the passage was left open and was only closed when people were inside the central chamber (Ashmore 1986: 57–62). By making the entrance lower, the builders of Maeshowe ensured that people entered its sacred space in a humble manner on their hands and knees.

THE NORTH-WEST AND NORTH-EAST BURIAL CHAMBERS

This picture shows two of the three small burial chambers and another of the four standing stones. The burial chamber to the right is directly facing through the cairn towards the rising hidden midsummer sun. The burial chamber to the left is generally aligned to where the hidden midsummer sun sets into a large enclosure on the higher ground; 490 metres to the north-west. Maeshowe would have been built around the internal markers that indicated the rising and setting sun, before any building began. Perhaps these were private ceremonies to the spirit ancestors in their burial cells, which were carried out as the hidden sun rose and set at midsummer and midwinter.

Crown copyright: HES

THE INNER ENTRANCE INTO MAESHOWE'S CENTRAL CHAMBER

The inner passage and two of the four internal standing stones that are placed at the corners of the main chamber. These standing stones were probably the first parts of the new monument to be built, and it is likely that they and the large stones forming the passage came from the stone circle that once stood here. All the four stones are carved with what might be faint Neolithic carvings which range from circular to triangular shapes (Ashmore 1984). The base of the right stone has the same Neolithic saltire symbols that are found above the entrance of Newgrange and at the Ness of Brodgar. As the stones are generally aligned towards the hidden rising midsummer sun and the setting midwinter sun, perhaps these are solar symbols. This of course would depend on them being carved on the stones when they were placed in this setting.
Crown copyright: HES

LOOKING ALONG MAESHOWE'S PASSAGE

Although the midwinter sun could not have shone directly into Maeshowe's central chamber, it would have been filled with its bright light. It is suggested that the importance of the sun to the builders of Maeshowe was not in defining the times of midwinter or of midsummer, but that it was connected with the ancestors in the small burial cells near these times. Hidden orientations to the sun and moon have been found in other monuments, such as Newgrange, and in some of the later Clava cairns. The evidence of the solar/lunar aligned monuments and buildings at the Ness of Brodgar, suggests a cooperative sophisticated society on Orkney, with links to Ireland. It would seem that these agrarian cultures throughout Europe shared religious beliefs that were linked through the ancestors with the energy of the sun and moon with the fertility of the earth. This also supports Dr Euan Mackie's idea that these societies 5,500 years ago, were run by some kind of astronomer priests.

Lewis

AERIAL VIEW OF CALANAIS FROM THE NORTH-WEST
NB 213330. LAT. 58° 11' N. LONG. 6° 44' 23" W

© Norman Strachan, 2016

CALANAIS TO THE NORTH

Looking north down the length of the northern avenue, with the central standing stone and remains of the burial cairn in the foreground. It is possible the cairn was built into the circle long after the stones were erected.

THE EASTERN CALANAIS STONE ROW

To the east the stones indicate where the sun and moon will rise near the equinoxes, Azi. 80°. Alt.1°. Decl. +6°.

THE WESTERN CALANAIS STONE ROW

On 21 March and September the equinox sun will set in line with the western alignment, Azi. 269°. Alt.0° 50'. Decl. 0°.

CALANAIS FROM THE NORTH-WEST

The Great Stones of Calanais

NO BOOK ABOUT Scotland's standing stones would be complete without including the great stones of Calanais on the island of Lewis. From a distance, they look like the skeletal backbone of a large dragon standing white against the blue of the sky. From above, they are shaped like a large Celtic cross. There is a tale that black men came to the island by boat and built the stones before sailing away. Another tale tells how 'the shining one', dressed in a cloak of bird feathers, would walk up the northern avenue to the circle at sunrise on midsummer's morning to the sound of a cuckoo.

The stones are made of white gneiss and they are absolutely stunning! They stand on a long northern-sloping hillside topped by a rock outcrop called the Cnoc an Tursa, on which is carved a single cup mark. From the egg-shaped stone circle, the remains of four stone rows radiate out to the north, east and west; the one to the south is aligned almost exactly to true north. The row to the south is focused towards the Clachan Tursa, and recent excavations have shown that fires had been lit within a small cave under this rock.

Just in front of the cave, a stone hole was found and it is likely that this held the southern most of the north-south row of standing stones. The focal point of Calanais is a massive standing stone that completely dominates the other 13 beautiful contorted stones of the circle. High up on the eastern side of this stone there is a single cup mark. At the base of the stone there are the remains of a passage cairn which is aligned towards the eastern horizon where the sun will rise near the spring and autumn equinoxes. A number of surveys have shown that the monument was aligned to the rising and setting sun and moon at different times (Thom, Ashmore, Pontings, Ruggles, and Scott).

From the centre of the circle, the eastern stone row points to where the sun or moon will rise about two weeks before the autumn and after the spring equinoxes, while the western row is aligned to where the equinox sun will set. The avenues could also have been used to look outward as well as in towards the circle. Looking south towards the circle from between the two stones at the end of the northern avenue, every 19–20 years at the major standstill, the midsummer full moon will arc low across the sky and will set into the circle near the base of the central standing stone.

CALANAIS AND THE MOON

Although it would be three years before the southern major standstill moon set at the base of the central stone, this picture of the setting moon as it passed in front of the centre stone was taken at about 10.30pm on 8 August 2003. The low moon that night was a deep red colour because it was seen through the Earth's atmosphere.

THE SOUTHERN VIEW OF CALANAIS

Looking south-south-west towards the circle from between the two stones at the northern end of the avenue.

North-East Scotland

TOM NAN CARRAGH, STRATHSPEY, NORTH-WEST VIEW
NJ 012 247. LAT. 57° 18' 3" N. LONG. 3° 39' 38" W

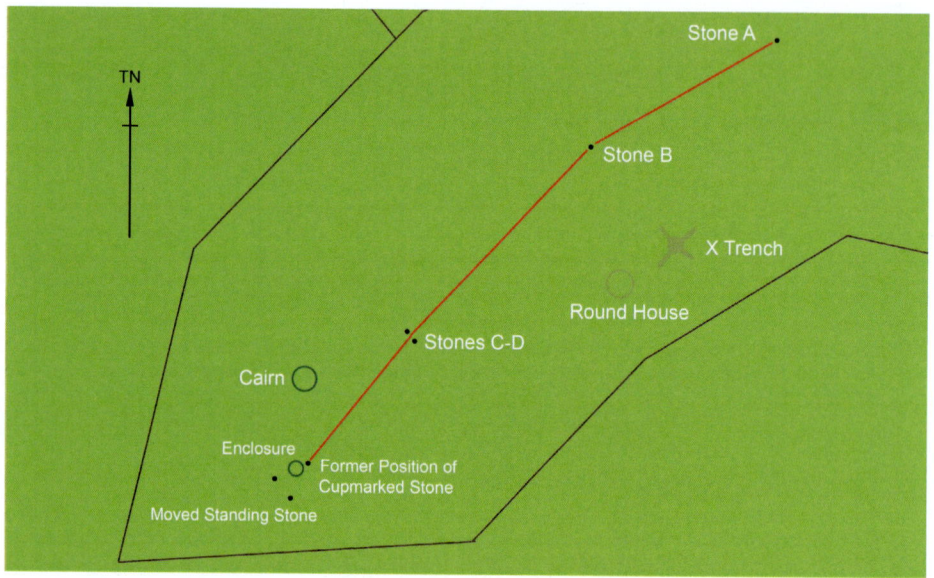

PLAN OF THE TOM NAN CARRAGH STANDING STONES

Showing the positions of the features and the sightline between the standing stones on Tom Nan Carragh.

Tom Nan Carragh, Strathspey

ON TOP OF Tom Nan Carragh (Hill of the Pillar) at Ballintomb farm, there are three 2.5-metre high standing stones A-B-D forming a 200-metre long north-east south-west line. Lying at the base of Stone D is Stone C, and an excavation showed that they once stood close together as a pair of standing stones. At the south-west end of the hill there is cup marked Stone E, lying in a natural semi-circular hollow. In 1986, the dairy farmer, Mr Simpson, showed Dougie where the cup marked stone had lain next to a small disturbed mound. A few metres south-west of this mound there is a 3-metre wide circular ditched enclosure. On the top of the hill there is a 5-metre wide low circular mound. Near the edge of the escarpment to the south-east of Stone B, there is a large, deep, cross-shaped feature, which is perhaps the remains of a burial cairn. A short distance to the south-west is the possible remains of a hut circle.

A Pictish Class 1 symbol stone now at Finlarig House was found when a farm cottage was demolished. The hill was the traditional gathering place of Clan Grant, where trials were held at the Figgat Fair in early May. As Tom Nan Carragh had been used from the Bronze Age to the 19th century, it is possible that the Pictish symbol stone was originally found on the hill. From the enclosure, Stones C–D and Stone B on the rising ground can be seen. Stone A is located on the lower ground about 100 metres to the north-east, and can only be seen from Stone B. From Stone A, only Stone B is visible. In June 2009, a shallow and narrow north-east trench was excavated from the centre of the small south-west circular enclosure by archaeologist Alistair Jupp, but only the 0.75-metre wide ditch and two post holes were found. The ditch was not excavated. Professor A. Thom proposed that the three standing stones marked the minor standstill moonset; however, my 1986 surveys suggest that Thom had assessed it remotely (Thom, A. Dulnainbridge, B7/3, p.119, 137, 1967).

From the south-west enclosure, Stones C–D and B generally indicated the midsummer sunrise. The cup marked stone would have generally marked the sunrise in early May and August. The positions of stones C–D suggest that they were originally set up to allow someone to stand between them to watch the midsummer sun rise in line with Stone B. From the same position, the sun could have been watched setting in line with Stone E near midwinter. From Stone B, Stones C–E are also generally aligned towards the midwinter sunset. From Stone B, the sun will rise above Stone A in early May and August. From Stone A, the sun will set in line with Stone B in early November and February (*Discovery and Excavation Scotland*, Pollock and Scott, D, 1988).

On 21 June 1987, from Stones C–D, the summer solstice sun was photographed rising just to the left of Stone B and, over the next 28 years, the sun was photographed rising and setting in line with the other stones. Although the stones do not accurately indicate the sun at the winter and summer solstices from Stones C–D, these turning times could have been known by simply counting the number of days before and after the sun rose in line with Stones B and E.

TOM NAN CARRAGH, STRATHSPEY

The south-west view of the Tom Nan Carragh standing stones (facing page) shows the locations of the three standing stones on the hill of Tom Nan Carragh. Tom Nan Carragh would originally have been surrounded on three sides by the flood waters of the nearby River Spey, and the area was drained when a large trench was cut across its north-east end during the 19th century.

THE VIEW SOUTH-WEST FROM STONES C-D

From Stones C–D, the midwinter sun set in line with the former position of the cup marked Stone E and the ditched enclosure at 3.00pm on 17 December 2002.

STONE B TO THE SOUTH-WEST

From the Stone B, the midwinter sun generally sets in line with stones C-D-E. There are a number of what appears to be small burial mounds scattered around this stone, suggesting that it was regarded as sacred.

STONE B TO NORTH-EAST STONE A

From Stone B, Stone A marks the rising sun in early May and August, some 45 days before and after the summer solstice. The stone can be seen to the lower right of the sun, and the sunrise was photographed at 4.45am on 8 May 2015, 28 years after Dougie's first visit here in 1986.

STONE A TO STONE B

As shown from Stone A at 4.00pm on 8 February 2003, the sun will set in line with Stone B on the hill in early February and November, Azi. 239°. Alt. 0° 45'. Decl. -15°. These times occur about 45 days before and after midwinter and were the later times of the Gaelic festivals of Samhain and Imbolc.

STONES C-D TO NORTH-EAST STONE B

The Midsummer sunrise at 4.30am from Stones C–D to Stone B, 1987.

The Recumbent Stone Circles

The recumbent stone circles of the Aberdeenshire area share similar architectural features with some of the Clava cairns around Inverness, such as cup marks and internal cairns surrounded by stone circles. They are also graded in height along their central axis, through the centre of the recumbent stone to the south or south-west to where the sun sets at midwinter, and in early November and February, and for the major standstill moon. Excavations have shown signs of burning and cremations at their centres, which suggests that this position was of importance. If the sun or moon were primary in rituals to the dead, this means that someone would have had to watch where they rose or set before the monument was built.

At Ardlair and Easter Aquhorthies circles, two large stones are placed at right angles to the inner side of the recumbent, and these are generally accepted as forming symbolic passages (Burl 1976: 179). These 'passage stones' were perhaps original features of these monuments which have since been removed, and their deliberate alignment suggests that the primary focus was between the flankers. The excavation of the Tomnaverie circle led Bradley to conclude that the recumbent was the last stone to be placed in position to close the monument (Bradley 2005, 2011).

This could therefore reflect the building sequence of the other recumbent circles, and would suggest that the sun or moon light was allowed to 'enter' the circle before it was closed. Surveys of the circles in the 1980s suggested that the midwinter sun and southern major and minor standstills moon set over the recumbent stones (Ruggles and Burl 1985). These surveys were unknown to Dougie, but they generally agreed with his assessment of some of these circles during the early 1990s. However, it is suggested that three of the circles, which were thought to be aligned to the southern minor standstill moon, were aligned to the setting sun in early November and February. Similar orientations have also been found at the Clava and Orkney-Cromarty passage cairns, and other monuments throughout Scotland (Scott, D. 2016). It is clear that the sun and moon were central to the beliefs of the builders of these monuments. Perhaps once the circles were closed the recumbents acted as spirit doors understood to be for the exclusive use of the sun or moon and the ancestors. The cremated bone found at their centres could perhaps suggests it was believed that this was where the ancestors 'lived'.

The sun was photographed at different times from a number of these circles. Due to their progressively lower horizons to the west, it was possible to photograph the setting sun from the Sunhoney, Midmar and Tomnaverie circles on 9 November 2014.

Sunhoney Recumbent Stone Circle

This circle is built below a range of high southern hills and is formed by 11 granite stones graded in height, south-west towards the high flanking stone on either side of the recumbent. Within the circle, there is a low raised circular bank, which is similar to those found inside some of the Clava ring cairns. The recumbent stone is lying to the inside of its two flankers, and it's difficult to understand how it could have ended up in its position if it had simply fallen. On its upper surface there are 35 cup marks, some of which are connected by angled grooves. The excavation showed the usual deposits of charcoal and cremated bone at the centre of the circle. A mile or so to the west is the Midmar Kirk recumbent stone circle.

Burl has proposed that the minor standstill full moon set in line with the recumbent stone every 19–20 years (Burl 1979: 145). From the centre of the circle the sun will set in line with its axis through the recumbent in early November and February, some 45 days before and after midwinter. The sun was photographed on 9 November 2014. It might be coincidental that the two flankers are aligned towards the midwinter sunrise and the setting midsummer sun. Given that the moon will set here during a minor standstill every 19–20 years, it would seem that the prime function for the monument was on the setting sun in early November and February.

This also occurs at the Midmar Kirk and Tomnaverie circles to the west. The south-western horizons of these three circles get progressively lower further to the west, so it was possible to visit each in turn on 9 November 2014 to photograph the sun setting in line with their recumbents. We know that these and many monuments were used for cremating or interring the dead, and were aligned to the sun and moon, but we do not know and can only speculate what this meant to these Neolithic or Bronze Age farmers.

SUNHONEY RECUMBENT STONE CIRCLE

THE CUP MARKS ON THE UPPER SURFACE OF THE RECUMBENT STONE

The simplest explanation for the position of the recumbent is that it fell apart before it could be raised and the flankers put in place. This can be seen in how the angled edges of the recumbent and right flanker are locked together. There are 27 cup marks on the centre of the recumbent, and these appear to be linked in some way with the setting sun, and perhaps the minor standstill moon. It might be just a coincidence that the flankers are aligned in the general directions of the rising midwinter and the setting midsummer sun. From the circle, the Midmar circle is located in the small wood on the skyline just in front of the right flanking stone, and the sun sets in line with it in early May and August.

THE RECUMBENT STONE FROM THE CENTRE OF THE CIRCLE

As shown at 2.58pm on 9 November 2014, the sun will set in line with the centre of the recumbent in early November and February. The midwinter sun would have set near the top of the hill to the left of the picture, and the moon near its southern major standstill moon would have briefly risen and set above the hill's left slope. The southern minor standstill moon would have set on the hill's lower right side every 19–20 years.

MIDMAR STONE CIRCLE, MIDMAR KIRK, GRAMPIAN
NJ 699064. LAT. 57° 9' N. LONG. 2° 30' W

Midmar Recumbent Stone Circle

Midmar Stone Circle is located a few kilometres to the west of Sunhoney, and it stands in the grounds of a modern graveyard of a church. Like many of these circles, the stones are graded in height towards the two flanking stones on either side of the massive recumbent. Because this circle is built on a slight slope, the shape of the recumbent was carefully chosen so that its upper surface would be horizontal. From Midmar, the midwinter sun and the southern moon can briefly rise and set on the southern horizon, but these directions were ignored and the recumbent stone was placed to face where the sun set on the south-west sloping horizon in early November and February. This will happen about 45 days before and after the winter solstice.

A similar use of the horizon can be seen at the recumbent stone circle of Stonehead, which is aligned to the setting midwinter sun. In the middle of the field to the west of the Midmar circle is a single standing stone, and although this might be a modern cattle rubbing stone, from the circle it points to where the sun will set near the spring and autumn equinoxes, 21 March to 21 September. Some 200m to the north-west of the circle on top of the hill is another large standing stone. Although it is now hidden by trees and may be the only remains of another circle, if this stone had been visible it could have been used to indicate the setting midwinter full moon at the major standstill. Even though the graveyard was only laid out in 1914, it is interesting to note that 4,500 years after these circles were used for the dead, the site still continues with this tradition.

THE RECUMBENT STONE SETTING FROM THE SOUTH

The shape of the recumbent was very carefully chosen to accommodate the slope of the hill. There is a single standing stone in the field to the west of the circle, and although it indicates the setting sun near the equinoxes, it is thought to be a cattle rubbing stone. Higher up the hill there is tall stone standing in a wood, but this might not have been visible from Midmar, and a survey showed that it is beyond where the midsummer sun or the northern moon can set.

THE RECUMBENT STONE FROM THE CENTRE OF THE CIRCLE

The sun setting above the recumbent at 3.14pm on 9 November 2014, on the western slope of the hill of Craigour, and this will occur again in early February. Azi. 233°. Alt. 3° 20'. Decl. -16°. The setting minor standstill moon will set on top of the hill, while the midwinter sun sets near the left flanker.

TOMNAVERIE STONE CIRCLE, GRAMPIAN
NJ486034. LAT. 57° 7' 9.97 N. LONG. 2° 50' 58" W

Tomnaverie Recumbent Stone Circle

This circle is located on top of a small hill and from it the cup marked recumbent stone faces the mountain of Lochnagar, 30 kilometres to the southwest. Like the hills of Tap O' Noth and Mither Tap, Lochnagar looks like a woman lying on her back. Fragments of beakers, flints, and quartz along with cremated human bone from a pit and a funeral pyre were found during its excavation. The circle was in a ruined state and it was fully restored after its excavation (Bradley 2005). Bradley comments:

Tomnaverie is one of a small group of sites whose orientation is well outside the segment of sky in which the sun appears. Ruggles had calculated that the monument could have been directed toward the moon every eighteen and a half years (Bradley 2005: 109–12).

The survey by Ruggles suggests that this was the minor standstill moon (Ruggles 1999, Tables 5.1–5.3: 212–5). However, the moon at this time will set well to the left of the top of Lochnagar. Bradley is mistaken that the sun cannot set between the flanker stones,

THE SETTING SUN FROM THE NORTH-EAST OF THE CIRCLE

The sun setting on top of Lochnagar at 3.44pm on the 9 November 2014. Azi. 237°. Alt. 1° 30'. Decl. -16°.

as Dougie's 1994 surveys and later photographs show that it will set on Lochnagar in early November and February.

After setting on Lochnagar in early November, the sun will continue to set to the left of the mountain each day until it reaches the left flanker around midwinter. After the winter solstice, the sun will start moving back along the horizon to the north and it will again set on Lochnagar in early February.

It is proposed that the circle was primarily aligned to the setting sun in early November and February, which are two of the eight divisions of the solar year.

These times are commonly found in the alignment of Neolithic and Bronze Age monuments throughout Scotland. Ruggles comments that the southern major standstill moon and the midwinter sun cannot rise above the height of the southern hills from the Sunhoney or Midmar recumbent stone circles (Ruggles 1999). Further surveys by Dougie show that the sun and moon can briefly rise above these horizons at these times, and this shows that there were other socio-religious reasons that the November and February times were chosen.

THE RECUMBENT STONE FROM THE CENTRE OF THE CIRCLE

The sun was at first hidden by cloud, but it later reappeared to the lower right at 3:53, before finally setting. The sun will set in line with the left flanker about midwinter, which is as far south as the sun can reach. Although the moon will set further to the left of the midwinter sun's position over the next four to five years until it reaches its southern major standstill position, no part of Tomnaverie is aligned in this direction.

Perthshire

VIEW OF CROFT MORAIG TO THE SOUTH-WEST
NN 797473. LAT. 56° 36' 6" N. LONG. 3° 57' 37"

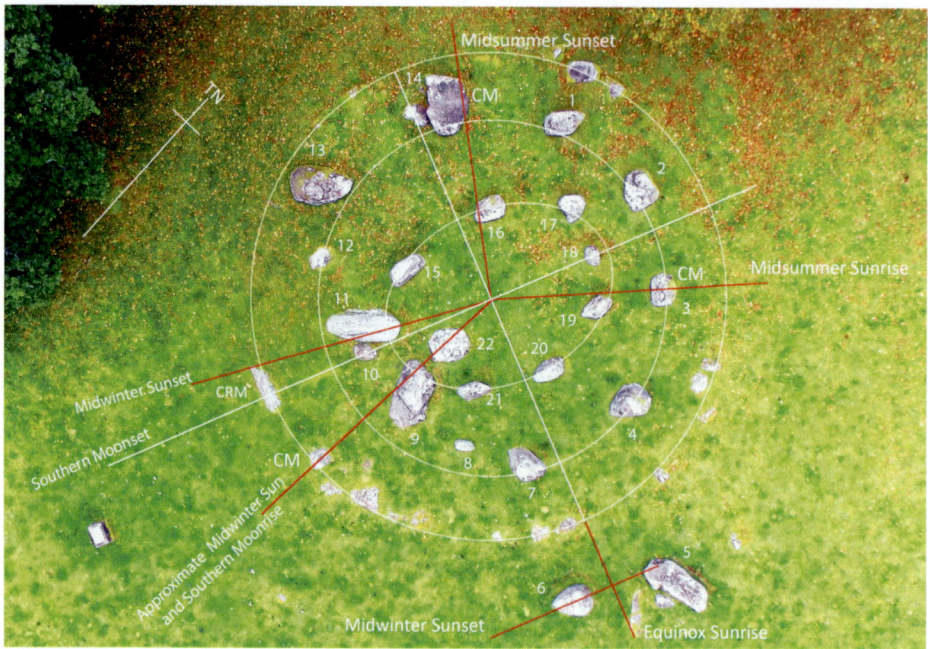

AERIAL VIEW OF CROFT MORAIG STONE CIRCLE

This aerial picture shows the solar and lunar orientations of the circle and its cup marked stones. The circle's long axis is aligned to where the moon sets near its southern major standstill. The lower red lines show the visible arc of the midwinter sun after it appears from behind the sloping horizon above the southern cup marked kerbstone before it passes over the top of the hill of Beinn Bhreac to set in line with the south-west cup and ring marked kerbstone. The upper red lines show the indications of the cup marked stones to the rising and setting midsummer sun.

Croft Moraig Stone Circle

THE CROFT MORAIG stone circle was built on an artificial platform on the edge of a slight slope and it is formed by a central oval of small standing stones graded in height to the south-west. These were surrounded in turn by nine large standing stones, a few of which have fallen, and an outer ring of low kerbstones. A number of the stones are cup marked and a south-west kerbstone is carved with cup and ring marks. The two eastern standing stones 5 and 6 were aligned to the south-west and north-east, and these were described as being a type of monument known as a Perthshire pair (Stewart 1964–6: 142).

The circle was excavated in 1965 by Piggott and Simpson, who proposed that a ring of wooden posts were the remains of a Neolithic building erected around a central buried stone, where fragments of bone, charcoal and quartz were found. The posts were replaced by the oval setting of stones and outer rings of standing stones and kerbstones (Piggott and Simpson 1971: 1–15). Bradley and Sheridan proposed a different building sequence for the circle, and it was dated to the middle Bronze Age. The mountain of Schiehallion was also thought to have held some significance for the circle (Bradley and Sheridan 2005).

During his 1992 survey, Dougie found five cup marks on the kerbstone to the south of the south-west cup and ring marked kerbstone. During the Bronze Age, the midwinter sun would have appeared from behind the sloping hillside to the upper left of the southern cup marked kerbstone. The sun would then have passed over the circle's axis to set in line with the south-west cup and ring marked kerbstone, and this was photographed on 10 December 2012. The moon, near but not at its southern major standstill, would have appeared to the upper right of the cup marked kerbstone, before setting in line with the circle's south-west axis, every 19–20 years. Cup marks were also found on the inner side of the north-east Stone 3, which indicated the midsummer sunrise. Although this was photographed on 7 July 2013, 17 days after the summer solstice, the sun would have moved only a short distance south in this time. All these surveys were shared with Prof. Bradley, who later credited Dougie in a 2005 paper with the finding that the midwinter sun set in line with the south-west cup and ring marked kerbstone (Bradley & Sheridan 2005). Dougie was curious about Bradley's interest in Schiehallion and a 2008 survey revealed that when the cup marked Stone 14 was standing, it would have indicated the midsummer sun just before it set behind the mountain. Professor Bradley was informed of this, and on 19 June 2016, he and Dougie met by chance at Croft Moraig, where they photographed the sun setting behind Schiehallion.

THE LONG SOUTH-WEST CUP AND RING MARKED KERBSTONE

This long kerbstone is carved with about 20 cup marks, two of which are ringed. It is possible that these symbols depict the midwinter sun and perhaps the southern moon as they set at different times on the high south-west horizon, Azi. 208°. Alt. 5°. Decl. -24°. This kerbstone is similar to the recumbent cup marked stone that was found in front of the false portal of the Culcarron kerb cairn and that of the Kintraw cairn in Argyll, which surveys show were also aligned to the midwinter sunset.

CUP MARKED KERBSTONE

Dougie found that this flat kerbstone had five plain cup marks on its outer edge in 1992. It lies a few metres to the south-east of the above cup marked stone and, from the centre of the circle, it is in line with where the setting moon and midwinter sun appear from behind the sloping southern horizon.

THE VIEW TO THE SOUTH-WEST

From the centre of the circle, the red line shows the approximate path of the Bronze Age winter solstice sun as it appears above the southern cup marked kerbstone, before passing over Beinn Bhreac, where it sets in line with the long cup and ring marked kerbstone, Azi. 208°. Alt. 5°. Decl. -24°. When standing, Stones 9 and 11 would have generally marked the setting midwinter sun. The white line shows where the southern full moon would approximately appear above the southern cup marked kerbstone before it set in line with the circle's axis every 19–20 years. The solar and lunar arcs were assessed from a photograph of stars that had the same sky positions of the midwinter sun and southern moon had during the Bronze Age. The moon will also set here in some of its other phases, Azi. 197°. Alt. 5°. Decl. -27°.

CROFT MORAIG STARS

The only way to show where the sun and moon set on the south-west horizon from Croft Moraig was by photographing the positions of the stars that today have about the same -24° declination as the sun had during the Bronze Age. This was assessed by using three faint stars in the constellations of Lepus and Eridanus in the above photograph that was taken at 7.38pm on 26 February 2019. The setting arc of the midwinter sun is approximately shown by the red line.

THE SETTING MIDWINTER SUN FROM CROFT MORAIG

The pictures on this page were taken at about 3.00pm on 10 December 2012, and they show the setting sun passing in line with Stone 10 and Stone 18 which form the axis of the circle, 11 days before the winter solstice. Most of the monuments are aligned to where the sun and moon rise and set. Similar combined solar/lunar orientations can be seen in the Druid temple, Carn Urnan and Avielochan Clava passage cairns near Inverness, aligned to the southern major standstill moon. Surveys show that their entrances were originally high enough to allow the midwinter sunlight to shine into the burial chambers (Scott, D. 2016).

THE LONG CUP AND RING MARKED KERBSTONE TO THE SOUTH-WEST

The setting midwinter sun from the long cup marked kerbstone, Azi. 208°. Alt. 5°. Decl. -24°. The two Newhall standing stones are located some 760 metres away behind the trees to the right, and they might have been visible from Croft Moraig, from which the sun will generally set near them around midwinter. These two Newhall stones are aligned to the setting midsummer sun, and although this has been photographed, this is not shown.

THE TWO EASTERN STANDING STONES TO THE SOUTH-WEST

Stone 5 has possibly fallen due to the excavation of the pit at its base in 1965, and it has the date 1846 carved on its upper surface. Like the circle, the stones were generally aligned towards the setting southern moon and the midwinter sun, and they have no solar or lunar alignment to the north-east.

NORTH-WEST VIEW FROM THE CENTRE OF THE CROFT MORAIG CIRCLE

At 9.24pm on 19 June 2013, while Professor Bradley took pictures of the midsummer sun setting behind Schiehallion from further up the hill, Dougie took them through the trees from the centre of the circle and the mountain is just to the right of the sun, Azi. 309°. Alt. 4° 20'. Decl. +23° 57'. The fallen cup marked Stone 14, can be seen in the background and Stone 16 is to the centre right.

NORTH-WEST VIEW OF SCHIEHALLION FROM THE HILL ABOVE THE CIRCLE

By the time Dougie got up the hill to Professor Bradley the sun had set behind Schiehallion. Similar to the Tap O' Noth and the Mither Tap in Aberdeenshire, the shape of the mountain looks like a female earth goddess and in Gaelic tradition it is the Maiden's Pap or the sacred Fairy Hill of the Caledonians. There are caves under the mountain and these were believed to lead deep into the underworld. Such beliefs could be rooted in the Bronze Age, and perhaps the midsummer sun setting behind the mountain was believed to be entering the Otherworld of the ancestors?

THE NORTH-EAST CUP MARKED STANDING STONE FROM THE CENTRE OF CROFT MORAIG CIRCLE

The sun rising above this north-east cup marked Stone 3 was photographed from the centre of the Croft Moraig stone circle at 5.10am on 7 July 2013. Although this was 17 days after midsummer, it shows that the midsummer sun would have originally risen above right side of this stone, Azi. 48°. Alt. 3° 20'. Decl. +24°.

The cup marks on Stone 3 are shown in white and it is possible that the lower line from right to left symbolises the rising moon moving along the horizon from its minor standstill to its major standstill, which will rise above the left side of the stone, Azi. 37°. Alt. 2° 30'. Decl. +28°. Croft Moraig might have been created to some venerated ancestor, whose remains may still lie under the buried centre stone. However, it is possible that the circle was built to watch where the sun and moon rose and set at the times described, and perhaps like the Temple Wood stone circle in Argyll, it was only later used as a burial monument.

MONZIE KERB CAIRN TO THE SOUTH-EAST
NN 882242. LAT. 56° 23' N. LONG. 3° 49' W

Monzie Kerb Cairn

The remains of this false portalled small kerb cairn are located in the parklands of Monzie Castle, surrounded by the beautiful Perthshire hills. A couple of hundred metres to the north-west, there is a small standing stone, which, from the cairn, is pointing towards the top of the mountain of Choinneachain (Kenneth's) Hill. The kerb cairn is graded in height south-south-west towards the highest pointed stone and cup and ring marked boulder. Other plain cup marks, some joined with grooves, can be seen on top of a south-east kerbstone.

An excavation in 1938 found some quartz fragments and cremated bone near the kerb cairn's centre. A rough path connected the kerb cairn to the cup and ring marked outlier, and there was no sign that this had ever been standing (Young and Mitchell 1939, vol. 73). The cremated bone was assessed as the remains of a woman and a child but, given the science of the time, this should be regarded with caution. Professor Alexander Thom's survey from the cairn to the north-west standing stone suggested that it indicated the midsummer sun setting on top of Kenneth's Hill (Thom 1967, P1/13. p.100). The HES aerial photographs show the crop images of what are thought to be a large enclosure to the west and two Pictish square barrows located between the north-west standing stone and kerb cairn.

Surveys and observations from the kerb cairn and the cup and ring marked boulder confirm that the north-west standing stone is indicating where the midsummer sun sets on Kenneth's Cairn on top of the mountain. The kerb cairn appears to be slightly oval in shape and its long axis is aligned with the outlying cup and ring marked slab to where the sun sets on Kate McNiven's Craig in early November and February.

The cup marked stone to the south-east of the circle is generally in line with the rising sun in early November and February. These solar orientations are likely to have had a symbolic function for the spirits of the dead. As there seems to be a solar connection between the cup and ring marked boulder, the kerb cairn and the standing stone, it is possible that the symbols around the edges of the outlier reflect the rising and setting sun as it moved towards the summer solstice position.

AERIAL VIEW OF MONZIE KERB CAIRN

Showing the general layout of the cup and ring marked outlier and the western aligned false portal of the kerb cairn.

THE SETTING SUN TO THE WEST FROM THE MONZIE KERB CAIRN

From the centre of the kerb cairn, the sun will set in line with its false portal near the equinoxes, as shown at 6:22pm on 25 March 2017.

MONZIE KERB CAIRN TO THE NORTH-WEST

A few hundred metres to the north-west there is a small standing stone that stands directly below the top of the mountain to the centre left of the photograph. Professor Thom's survey suggested that the stone indicates the midsummer sun setting on top of the hill of Choinneachain, where there is a large burial cairn, Azi. 307°. Alt. 4° 50'. Decl. +23° 30'. It is likely from the fragments found at the base of the kerbstones that the cairn was covered in a layer of white quartz.

KATE MCNIVEN'S, OR, THE WITCHES STONE

The outlying north-west standing stone is named after Kate McNiven, who was said to have been tied to the stone and burnt as a witch, but there is no proof that she ever existed. Perhaps she was a faint memory of the Cailleach, whose spirit was believed to live inside the standing stone.

THE WITCHES STONE TO THE SOUTH-WEST

The standing stone, known locally as the Witches Stone, is leaning slightly, and its distinctive flat side is also aligned, like the circle and its cup and ring marked slab, to the setting sun in early November and February.

THE CUP AND RING MARKED STONE AND KERB CAIRN TO THE NORTH-EAST

This is one of the most highly decorated stones in Scotland and it is carved with a profusion of beautiful rock art. Like most cup and ring marks, the radial grooves run down from the central cups. From this stone the northern midwinter full moon will rise in line with the ring cairn during a major standstill, Azi. 49°. Alt. 7'. Decl. +27° 30', and the midsummer sun will rise on the flat topped hill in the background, Azi. 60°. Alt. 9'. Decl. +23 40'. It is possible that these symbols were used in rituals to the ancestors as the sun rose and set over the Perthshire hills. The two cup and ring marks on the stone are joined and form a proto Double Discs symbol.

THE MONZIE CUP AND RING MARKED STONE FROM ABOVE

The top of the picture is to the south-west.

KATE McNIVEN'S CRAIG TO THE SOUTH-WEST OF THE KERB CAIRN

At 2.47pm on 2 November 2017, the sun was photographed setting in line with the cairn's tallest kerbstone and cup and ring marked outlier on Kate McNiven's Craig.

THE KERB CAIRN TO THE NORTH-WEST

The sun will set on the mountain top for about a week before and after the summer solstice and this was first photographed at 5.00pm on 25 June 2001. The cremated remains found within the circle suggest that this and the other solar orientation had a ritual function for the dead, rather than an astronomical one. Given the close proximity of the large carved slab to the burial cairn, the main orientation is probably to the November or February sunsets.

ROMAN STONE, PERTHSHIRE
NN 774260. LAT. 56° 21' 43" N. LONG. 3° 59' 7" W

VIEW FROM THE CUP MARKED STONE TO THE SOUTH-WEST ROMAN STONE

From the cup marked stone, the sun set in line with the Roman Stone at 3.46pm on 2 November 2017 and the shadow of the standing stone moved slowly over the 22 cup marks. These orientations to the sun at these times are commonly found at other Neolithic and Bronze Age monuments in Scotland. Although the cup marked slab might have been moved, this is how Fred Coles first described them over 100 years ago (Coles 1911: 59).

The Roman Stone

About a mile to the south of Comrie just off the main road to Stirling is the Roman Stone, which has a line of two boulders a short distance to the north-east, with the latter stone being carved with 22 cup marks. The Roman Stone is so called because it stood within the walls of a later Roman fort. Comrie is prone to small earthquakes, and perhaps over the millennia these have caused the stone to lean over. A survey in the 1990s suggesting that the sun would set in line with these stones in early November and February was confirmed on 2 November 2017.

Cloanlawers

Some 400 metres above Loch Tay on the southern slopes of Meall Greigh, there is a large, natural, 2-metre high standing stone, which, from a number of nearby cup marked stones, indicates the rising moon and the rising and setting midsummer sun. This survey information was later shared with and used by Professor Richard Bradley who had previously excavated four of these cup marked rocks (Bradley & Watson 2007–10, 2012).

The recent excavations of these cup marked sites are invaluable in helping us to understand how and when the cup marks were made. This, however, does not tell us why they were created. The surveys of cup marks on monuments show that they were connected in some way with the sun and moon (Scott, D. 2003, 2010, 2016). Spirals are especially associated with the midwinter-aligned monuments such as Newgrange in Ireland, the Long Meg stone circle in Cumbria, and at the end of a line of monuments on Cambret Moor in Galloway. A further insight into their use can perhaps be gained by looking at the ethnographic record of other cultures. Many ancient cultures believed in

THE NATURAL STANDING STONE AT CLOANLAWERS
NN 69073 42737. LAT. 56° 33' N. LONG. 4° 7' 52.72" W

a three-tiered cosmology of heaven, Earth and the underworld, which could have spread throughout the world as our ancestors left Africa 150,000 years ago. All hunter-gatherer cultures had shamans who believed that they could interact with the spirits inhabiting these realms, and such beliefs are still practised today. Freuchen comments that there are a number of ways of slipping in and out of trances, and describes one way the Inuit shamans do this:

Another way is to obtain concentration and paralysis of the conscious mind by, for instance, going to a lonely place and rubbing a stone in a circle on a rock for hours and days on end. On achieving this altered state of consciousness, they believed they could actually travel to the underworld where they would meet with their ancestors or the spirit guides of the sun and moon. (Freuchen 1961 p.213)

Gifts of meat were given to the great spirit Torngarsuk, the master of the earth, to thank him for his hospitality.

These beliefs are a continuity from our Paleolithic and Mesolithic ancestors, who saw nature as the manifestation of powerful spirits, which over time evolved into the families of gods in other cultures throughout the world. Some aspects of the ritual use of cup marks seem to have survived in remote areas of the British Isles until the late medieval period. In Gaelic Scotland and Ireland, cup marks or Clachan Aoradh (worship stones) were used to hold offerings of food or drink to spirits called the Tuatha dé Danann, or the Sidhe (shee) as they were also known. Stones were also turned within cup marks to placate and contact the Sidhe, who were believed to inhabit cairns and cup marked rocks to ensure the health and fertility of crops and cattle. As these spirits lived in burial cairns, it is proposed that they are a cultural memory of those we call the ancestors (Scott, D. 2016).

In Scandinavia, these fertility spirits were known as the elves, and gifts of milk were left in cup marks to thank them for the harvests (Davidson 1964). The

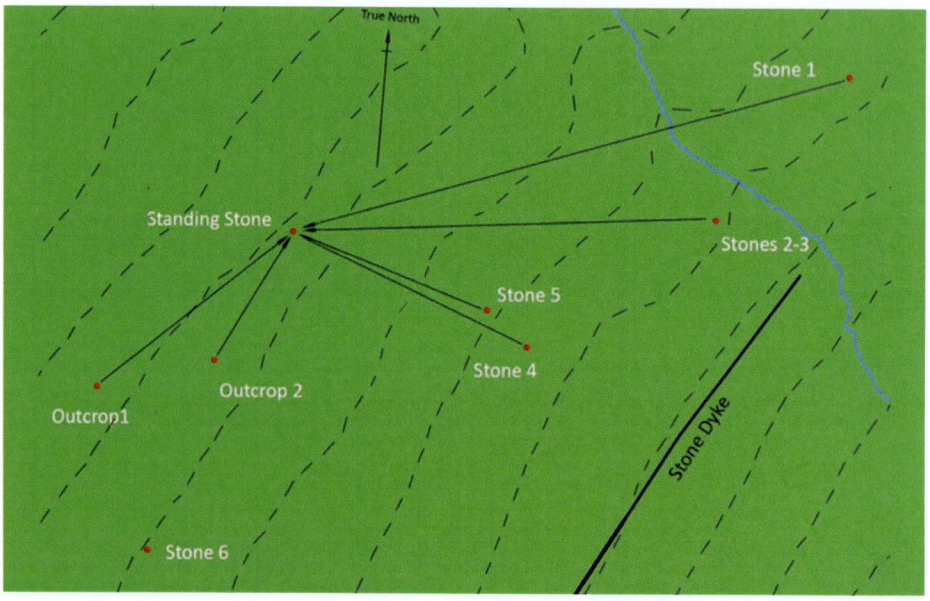

MAP OF THE CUP MARKED STONES AT CLOANLAWERS

Showing the location and proposed solar/lunar orientations of the Cloanlawers cup marked rocks. The stones are numbered in sequence from the north-east to the south-west and some photographs of the rising and setting sun and moon are shown in the following pages. The illustration is for visual reference only and the following solar/lunar orientations and dates derived from the surveys should be treated as being approximate.

leaving of food for the ancestors at cup marked rocks and burial monuments was also common throughout the world. The Inuit shamans believed that, in a trance state, their spirits could swim through the rocks to the underworld (Freuchen 1961: 210). Drawing on the living traditions of Madagascar, similar ideas of spirits in standing stones have also been suggested by archaeologists Ramilisona and Mike Parker Pearson. This would suggest that the cup and ring marks on Meall Greigh, and at other sites scattered throughout the country, were ritually used to contact the ancestors as the sun or moon rose out of or set into the Otherworld.

THE SOUTHERN VIEW FROM THE CUP MARKS ON OUTCROP 2.
From the hollow, the cup marks on this part of Outcrop 2 might reflect the major standstill moon rising out of the hill and arching across the southern horizon before setting.

THE STANDING STONE TO THE SOUTH-WEST

Professor Bradley excavated the base of this stone and concluded that it was natural, but he has suggested that such features were sometimes ritually used in the prehistoric past. The flat side of the stone is aligned towards Outcrop 2, above which the midwinter sun set. Outcrop 1 is slightly further up the hill and is hidden behind the stone.

THE NORTH-EAST VIEW FROM OUTCROP 2 TO THE 'STANDING STONE'

From the cup marks on the upper part of Outcrop 1, the midwinter major standstill full moon will rise to the upper right of the 'standing stone' every 19–20 years. For example, this would have occurred at 3.21pm on 5 January 2090 BC, Azi. 39°, Alt. 2° 50', Decl. + 28°.

BRANCHING CUP AND RING MARKS AT THE BASE OF OUTCROP 1

The four faint cup and ring marks at the base of the outcrop are connected with branching grooves.

THE LARGE CUP AND RING MARK TO THE NORTH-EAST

From the cup and ring mark, the 'standing stone' now indicates the midsummer sun rise, Azi. 46°. Alt. 0° 40'. Decl. +24°. The picture shows the midsummer sun at about 4.40am on 25 June 2012, as it briefly appeared through the cloud shortly after it had risen.

THE GROOVE OF THE LARGE CUP AND RING MARK ON OUTCROP 1 IS ALIGNED TO THE NORTH-WEST

The large cup and ring mark on Outcrop 1 appears to be surrounded by an outer ring which curves off to the north and connects with a natural crack in the rock.

THE LARGE CUP AND RING MARK TO THE SOUTH-EAST

From the cobbled area the spiralled cup and ring mark is generally in line with the midwinter sunrise. The curving outer end of the spiral runs into a large, natural, quartz-filled crack, seen here at the bottom of the picture. Perhaps each cup mark of the 'ring' of cup marks symbolises the general position of the sun or moon as they rose and set around the horizon.

THE NORTH-WEST VIEW FROM THE LARGE CUP AND RING MARK ON OUTCROP 1

The symbol's groove is aligned in the general direction of the setting midsummer sun, as shown at 7.36pm on 19 June 2013. The four cup and ring marks at the base of the outcrop are connected with branching grooves which are focused upwards towards the spiral. This could suggest that the spiral on top of the outcrop symbolised the sun setting on the mountain.

THE UPHILL NORTH-WEST VIEW FROM STONE 4

The two grooved cup and ring marks on the triangular area on the eastern side of Stone 4 are difficult to see. They are aligned uphill towards the standing stone, above which the midsummer sun set at 7.43pm on 19 June 2013, Azi. 290°. Alt. 16°. Decl. +24°. Shortly after this, Dougie met up with Professor Richard Bradley at the Croft Moraig stone circle, where they watched the lower midsummer sun set behind the mountain of Schiehallion.

THE LARGE CUP AND RING MARKS ON STONE 6

These remarkable carvings on Stone 6 can be found about 100 metres downhill to the south of Outcrop 1. They comprise two large cup and ring marks with another two smaller symbols below the left cup and ring mark. The lower rings of the right symbol are unfinished.

THE UPHILL VIEW FROM STONE 6

From this position, the standing stone is too far to the north to indicate the sun or moonrise. However, just like those on Stone 5, these radial grooves are also generally aligned to the sun setting along the horizon throughout the summer. The picture shows the sunset at 6.30pm on 23 July 2011.

THE STANDING STONES AT EAST CULTS
NO 0725 4216. LAT. 56° 33' 44" N. LONG. 3° 30' 39" W

On top of the hill near East Cults Farm, two standing stones forming a 10-metre east–west alignment are aligned to the rising and setting sun near the equinoxes, 21 March – 21 September. To the west, Azi. 266°. Alt. 2° 40'. Decl. 0°, and to the east, Azi. 86°. Alt. 0°. Decl. + 2°. A third stone lying nearby with about 150 cup marks on its upper surface might be the remains of a fallen standing stone.

THE CUP MARKED STONE AT EAST CULTS

This wedge shaped stone may be all that remains of a third standing stone that once stood in line with the other two stones. The cup marks could also have been used in connection with the rising and setting sun near the spring and autumn equinoxes

GENERAL VIEW OF EAST CULTS STANDING STONES TO THE WEST

This picture was taken from just to the south of the line between the standing stones to show the setting equinox sun at 5.55pm on 20 September 1992.

THE CLEAVEN DYKE, PERTHSHIRE TO THE NORTH-WEST
NO 1633 4049. LAT. 56° 32' 56" N LONG. 3° 21' 42" W

The Cleaven Dyke

The Cleaven Dyke near Blairgowrie is a 3-kilometre-long Neolithic monument, which is formed by a central earth bank and two parallel ditches, 20 metres on either side. At its north-west end, there is what appears to be a large burial mound. The early antiquarians thought the Dyke had been built by the Romans, yet excavations dated its construction to the Neolithic Period some 5,500 years ago (Barclay 1993–8). The Dyke is aligned in both directions to the rising sun in early May and August and the setting sun in early November and February. As shown on the opposite page, these events were photographed at 8.38pm on 4 May 2017, and 8.37am on 29 October 2017. Ruggles dismisses that the Dyke was deliberately aligned to these times as it could have been orientated towards a hill near where the midsummer sun set (Barclay 1993–8). Dougie's surveys of the Orkney-Cromarty cairns has shown that they were commonly orientated towards the sun in early November and February.

THE CLEAVEN DYKE TO THE NORTH-WEST

The sun setting in line with the Dyke at 8.38pm on 4 May 2017.

THE CLEAVEN DYKE TO THE SOUTH-EAST

The sun rising in line with the Dyke above Lethendy Hill at 8:37am on 29 October 2017.

THE ORWELL STONES TO THE SOUTH-EAST
NO 1494 0432. LAT. 56° 31' 49.27" N. LONG. 4° 9' 27" W

The Orwell Standing Stones

THE ORWELL STANDING STONES TO THE EAST

These two stones stand some 13 metres apart to the north-west and south-east of each other. Fred Coles describes that bones were found near the stones in the 19th century (Coles 1906: 293). The north-east pointed stone had fallen; before it was re-erected, Graham Ritchie's excavations in 1972 found cremated bone at the base of each stone (Ritchie 1974: 27). Graham and Dougie visited and surveyed the stones in the early 1990s and this showed that to the south-east and north-west, they marked the rising and setting sun in early November and February and May and August. It would seem from this that their solar orientations were for the spirits of the dead. The pictures show the sunrise at 4.40am on 2 November 2018.

As the beautiful sun rose in line with the Orwell standing stones, large flocks of geese took to the frosty skies. The Lomond Hills to the east looked like a giant Earth Goddess giving birth to the sun at the time of the Gaelic festival of Samhain. The sun will also rise in line with the stones in early February, some 45 days after midwinter, at the time of the later festival of Imbolc that was dedicated to the spring goddess, Bride. There is a Gaelic saying that 'The Goddess Bride leaves her cairn at this time to bring life back to the earth after the death time of winter'. Similar solar events occur from the Ardlair stone circle to the hill of the Mither Tap in Aberdeenshire. In the opposite direction, the sun setting in line with the stones in early May and August, marks the festivals of Beltane and Lughnasad.

Argyll

THE KINTRAW STANDING STONE TO THE SOUTH-WEST
NM 830050. LAT. 56° 12' N. LONG. 5° 31' W

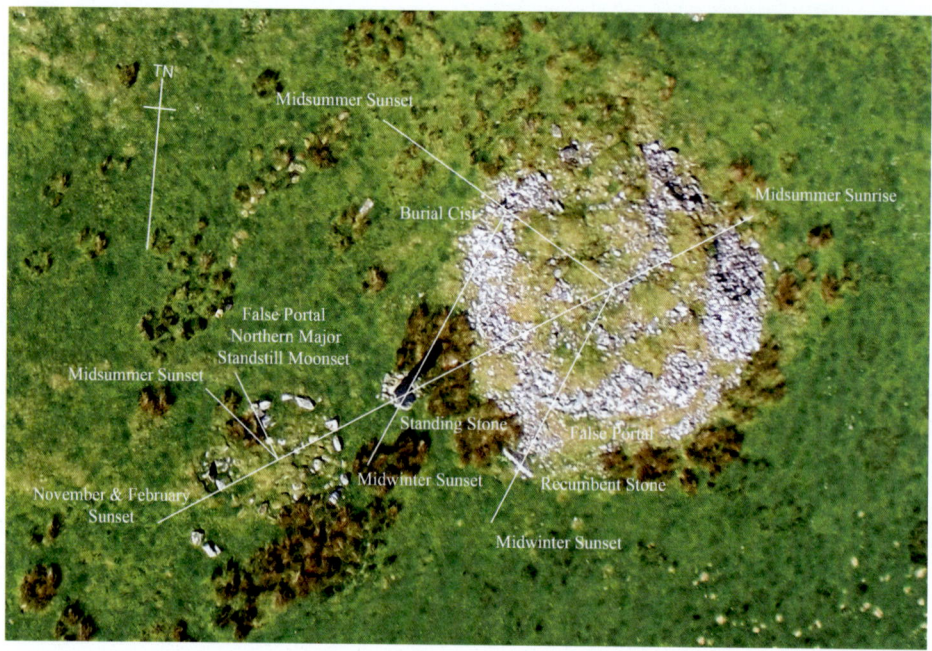

AERIAL VIEW OF THE MONUMENTS AT KINTRAW, ARGYLL

This aerial picture shows the solar/lunar orientations of the Kintraw monuments. Aubrey Burl's suggestion that the two cairns were in line with the midsummer sunrise was confirmed by Dougie's photograph, taken at about 4:30am on 10 June 2002. Dougie found that the cairns to the south-west were aligned to the setting sun in early November and February, and this was photographed on 5 November 2005. The position of the smaller cairn's burial cist is the dark green patch of grass on its north-west side, and this is in line with the midsummer sunset. Just next to this are the remains of an unknown small false portal, which aligns with where the northern major standstill moon sets every 19–20 years.

The Kintraw Cairn

ON A HILLSIDE TERRACE overlooking the northern end of Loch Craignish at Kintraw, there is a large stone standing between two burial cairns. A drawing by Edward Lhuyd from 1699 shows the two cairns and standing stone, with another large circular flat-topped monument to the north-west, which can still be seen today. The large north-east burial cairn appeared to have an entrance on its south-west side. The ring of stones can still be seen, and two large boulders are perhaps the remains of the four stone alignment. The large cairn appeared to have an entrance on its south-west side.

When Simpson excavated the cairns in 1959–60, he discovered that Lhuyd's entrance in the larger cairn was a false portal. In front of this was a long recumbent stone that was surrounded by quartz. The cairn had no central burial, but a wooden post had once stood at its centre. A burial cist on the north-west side of the cairn was found to contain some fragments of cremated bone and some burnt wood. Apart from a small burial cist containing pieces of burnt wood, nothing was found in the smaller cairn (Simpson 1968: 54–9). The standing stone fell in 1978 and nothing was found when it was excavated (Cowie 1979). When the stone was re-erected in its original position, it was realigned in the wrong

KINTRAW CAIRN AND STANDING STONE TO THE NORTH

The standing stone and cairn with the long recumbent stone in front of the false portal, which was unfortunately reburied after the excavation. Many of these burial cairns were originally covered with fragments of quartz, and this probably explains why in Gaelic some of them are called Cairnbaan, the White Cairn.

direction, in line with the two cairns. A picture taken before the stone fell shows it was aligned towards the high south-southwest horizon. Burl has suggested that the large cairn's false portal was perhaps in line with the major standstill moon set on this high horizon (Burl 1976: 199).

Surveys and observations from the centre of the cairn show that the midwinter sun set in line with the recumbent stone, which presumably still lies in front of the reburied false portal. The midwinter orientation of Kintraw's false portal is similar to that of the Culcharron cairn in Benderloch, in front of which a cup marked slab was found. Also in Benderloch, the passage of the Cairnbaan cairn is aligned towards the midwinter sunrise. From the centre of the large Kintraw cairn, the standing stone marks where the sun sets in early November and February, while the midsummer sun sets in line with the north-west burial cist. From this burial cist, the standing stone marks where the midwinter sun set on the high south-west horizon. Burl's suggestion that, from the small cairn, the standing stone marked the midsummer sunrise was confirmed by a photograph taken at 5.00am on 10 June 2002.

Perhaps the false portal was built because the horizon where the midwinter sun sets is high and its light could not have entered a level passage into a burial chamber. Yet, it is obvious from their alignment that the false portal, the standing stone and the burial cist were vital to the cairn builder's solar beliefs. Professor Thom proposes that after the cairn was built where the southern half of the Jura notch was hidden by Dun Arnal, it was then decided to mark the notch with the standing stone and watch the sunset from a higher northern hillside terrace. This terrace is possibly a disused farm track. Dr Euan MacKie's 1970–1 excavation found several large stones on the terrace, but there was no archaeological evidence to date it to the Bronze Age (MacKie 1977).

KINTRAW, SOUTH-WEST VIEW FROM THE BURIAL CIST

The above picture was taken from the north-west burial cist as the midwinter sun set in line with the standing stone at 2.15pm on 19 December 2003, Azi. 204°. Alt. 7°. Decl. -23° 24. A passage could have aligned towards the sun near the bottom of the hill slope a few days before the winter solstice, but this area was avoided and the higher horizon was chosen.

THE LEANING KINTRAW STANDING STONE IN 1977

Taken in thick mist from the north-west burial cist in 1977, this picture shows how the stone's flat side was originally aligned south-west towards the large eastern kerbstone of the smaller cairn. There is a vertical line of eroded natural holes on the flat western side of the stone, and some of the lower hollows could be cup marks. The stone fell that year, but when re-erected and set in concrete, it was realigned in the wrong directions along the axis between the two cairns. From the burial cist, the eastern kerbstone shows that the stone was originally aligned towards the midwinter sunset on the high south-west horizon.

VIEW FROM THE CENTRE OF KINTRAW CAIRN TOWARDS THE SOUTH-WEST FALSE PORTAL

From the centre of the cairn the midwinter sun set on the high horizon in line with the false portal on the 19 December 2002. After the sun had set, its top half was photographed as it reappeared about an hour later halfway down the hill slope where it was hidden by clouds.

THE PAPS OF JURA FROM THE NORTH-WEST OF THE CAIRN

Professor Thom's suggestion that the upper edge of the winter solstice sun set in the Jura notch was flawed from the very start, as why would its builders have placed the cairn where the notch could not be seen? Thom says the notch can be seen from just to the north of the cairn, but states his proposed solar event would not have been visible from this position. If the sun actually set in the notch at this time, given that it is 29 miles away, it is highly likely that it would have been visible. After photographing the midwinter sunset at the Ballymeanoch stones on 19 December 2003, Dougie stopped at the Kintraw cairn on the way home. Someone there showed him a video they had taken shortly before of the sun's disc as it set in a cloudless sky on top of Dun Arnal. Given that the winter solstice sun originally set further to the left, this suggests that the cairn builders had no interest in the Jura notch and that Thom had come up with the hillside terrace to fit his theories.

KINTRAW STANDING STONE TO THE SOUTH-WEST, FROM THE CENTRE OF THE LARGE CAIRN

From the centre of the large burial cairn the sun set in line with the standing stone at about 5pm on 5 February 2005 and this will also happen in early November – the times of the Gaelic festivals of Bride/Imbolc and Samhain. Azi.138°. Alt.1°20'. Decl.-16°. The festival of Samhain, today called Halloween, is when the Sidhe spirit ancestors could return to the world for one night.

VIEW ALONG THE NORTH-EAST AXIS OF THE THREE MONUMENTS

From the centre of the smaller south-western burial cairn, the midsummer sun rose in line with the standing stone at 5.00am on 10 June 2002, Azi. 58°. Alt. 8'. Decl. +24°. This event was also videoed and the orientation should only be regarded as general as the sun will rise in line with the stone for about a week on either side of the summer solstice.

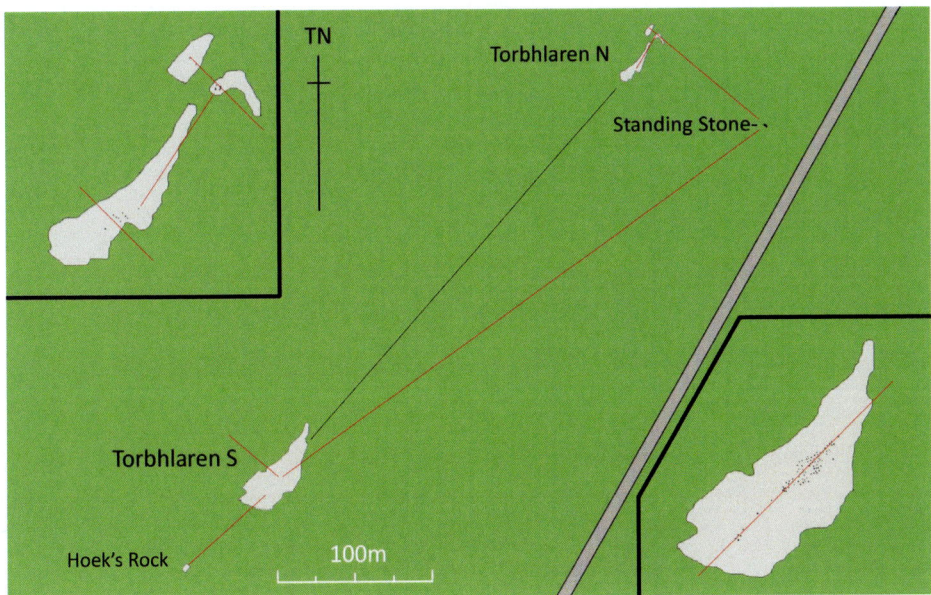

THE POSITION OF TORBHLAREN STANDING STONE AND THE CUP MARKED OUTCROPS

The sightlines on and between the Torbhlaren North and Torbhlaren South carved rock outcrops.

Torbhlaren, Argyll

In the Kilmichael Glen, there are two cup and ring marked rock outcrops, Torbhlaren North and South, which are located some 200 metres north-east and south-west of each other (Campbell and Sanderman PSAS 1961; Morris and Thomson DES 1969). The carvings on Torbhlaren North are located at the central and northern areas of the outcrop, while on Torbhlaren South they are on its flat top. To the south-west of this, a few cup and ring marks were found on a small area of bedrock by rock art researcher Maarten van Hoek (Maarten van Hoek DES 1980).

Ronald Morris commented that the farmer, Mr Thomson, had found a fallen standing stone and some fragments of flint to the north-west of Torbhlaren South. The original position of this stone is unknown, as it was moved shortly afterwards to bridge a small stream to the south-west of the Torbhlaren South (Morris 1977). The general north-west location of the stone was confirmed during a conversation Dougie had with Mr Thomson in 1978. In 2012, Dougie noticed that the flat upper surface of this stone was carved with three long and six short shallow straight grooves which created squared shapes. To the south-east of Torbhlaren North, there is a 1.8-metre-high standing stone with a number of cup marks on its lower southern and northern sides.

The stone is leaning slightly to the north-east and a survey of its flat side in 1985 found that, when upright, it was aligned towards the midsummer sunset. The orientation of the rock art on these outcrops and to the standing stone suggested that they mark where the sun or moon will rise and set at different times within the eight divisions of the Bronze Age calendar.

Dougie photographed the sun rising near the standing stone from Torbhlaren South in 2002.

TORBHLAREN STANDING STONE TOWARDS THE TORBHLAREN NORTH OUTCROP
NR 863944. LAT. 56° 5' N. LONG. 5° 25' W

The Torbhlaran standing stone is leaning slightly to the north and the above photograph, taken at 8.59pm on 20 June 2012, shows that its flat southern side is aligned towards the setting midsummer sun, Azi. 307°. Alt. 7° 30'. Decl. +24°. During the Bronze Age, the slightly higher midsummer sun would have set further to the right above the cup and ring marks on the northern end of the Torbhlaran rock outcrop. The sun will also set above the cup and ring marks at the centre of the outcrop in early May and August. The Torbhlaran standing stone has about 34 cup marks on its southern side, some of which are connected by grooves, and there are nine cup marks of the northern side of the stone, which might have once stood in line with another standing stone.

Dr Andy Jones' excavations from 2002–8 found that low clay platforms had been built around the two Torbhlaren outcrops and that these were covered with fragments of quartz. Broken quartz and hammer stones were also found below the cup marked areas, and were thought to have been used to carve the rock. It has also been proposed that Mr Thomson's fallen standing stone was found to the south-west of Torbhlaren South (Jones 2011). This is at odds with its north-west location mentioned by Morris.

SOUTHERN SIDE OF TORBHLAREN STANDING STONE

VIEW TO THE NORTH-WEST FROM THE CENTRAL PANEL ON TORBHLAREN NORTH OUTCROP

The rock panel of worn cup and ring marks is aligned to where the northern major standstill moon will set on the north-west horizon every 19–20 years. However, as the panel is fixed, it is possible that the symbols might have represented the midsummer sun as it set further to the right during the Bronze Age. The picture was taken at 8.55pm on 20 June 2012. The rock panel to the right is smooth, but it was not carved.

VIEW FROM THE CUP AND RING MARKS AT THE NORTHERN END OF TORBHLAREN NORTH OUTCROP TOWARDS THE SOUTH-EAST STANDING STONE

Taking advantage of the cold clear weather, Dougie went to Torbhlaran on the 2 February 2013, and at 9.36 am he photographed the rising sun from the cup and ring marks. Although this was a few days early, it shows that the sun would rise above the standing stone about 6 February and November, Azi. 138°. Alt. 9° 45'. Decl. -16°.

SOUTH-WEST VIEW ALONG TORBHLAREN SOUTH

The former standing stone found to the north-west of Torbhlaren South now lies over a small burn 140 metres to the south-west of the outcrop, Lat. 56° 5' 36. 56" N. Long. 5° 26' 25.12" W. Its upper side is carved with shallow grooves creating irregularly sized square shapes. From the north-east, the midwinter sun setting above the cup and ring marks on the highest part of the outcrop at 3.02pm on 25 December 2014 suggested that this was the focus of these south-west cup marks. If Morris gave the wrong location for the fallen standing stone, perhaps from the outcrop it marked the midwinter sunset.

AERIAL VIEW OF THE TOP OF TORBHLAREN SOUTH

The carvings run along the outcrop's flattest area, approximately aligned towards the midwinter sunset. The sun at this time would have originally set just to the left of the dome shape outcrop on the south-west horizon, directly above some cup and ring marks located on Torbhlaren's highest point.

NORTH-EAST VIEW FROM TORBHLAREN SOUTH TO TORBHLAREN NORTH AND STANDING STONE

At around 4.30am on 10 June 2002, the midsummer sun was photographed from Torbhlaren South as it briefly appeared through the clouds. It is therefore possible that the cup marks on the outcrop were created as the sun rose in the weeks before or after the summer solstice. If the Torbhlaren North standing stone once formed an alignment with another stone, perhaps it indicated the midsummer sunrise from Torbhlaren South. The rows of symbols are aligned north-east towards the Torbhlaren North standing stone above which the sun will rise in early June. The Torbhlaren South outcrop is aligned towards Torbhlaren North above which the northern major standstill moon will rise every 19–20 years. It is therefore possible that the rows of cup marks are reflecting rituals to the sun around midsummer and to the northern moon. Shortly after this Dougie went to Kintraw and photographed the midsummer sun rising in line with the standing stone.

TORBHLAREN SOUTH FROM SOUTHERN CUP AND RING MARKED BOULDER

From the cup and rink marked bedrock found by Maarten van Hoek, it is possible to show, by comparing the position of the midsummer sun in the picture above, that the summer solstice sun would have appeared to rise out of the cup and ring marks on top of Torbhlaran South during the Bronze Age.

AERIAL VIEW OF THE UPPER CAIRNBAAN CUP AND RING MARKS

Symbols higher up the hill are carved on an area of bedrock that slopes uphill to the north-west, while most of their radial grooves run down the rock into natural cracks. The three upper symbols are joined through their central cups by a horizontal groove, and these connect with the lower three symbols in a sinuous line. These symbols to the north-east and south-west are generally aligned towards the rising midsummer and the setting midwinter sun.

Cairnbaan Rock Art

The cup and ring marks at Cairnbaan are carved on large sheets of sloping bedrock, which are located near the top of a hill above the Cairnbaan Hotel. The lower strip of bedrock is aligned to the north-east and south-west and gently slopes down to south-east, with the symbols being carved into panels formed by horizontal cracks. The upper group of the symbols can be found 100 metres further up the hill, carved on a large area of bedrock which also slopes down from the north-west to south-east. Towards the top of the bedrock are three horizontally placed ring symbols, with two actually touching each other. The rest of the rings form a sinuous line shaped like the number two, which finishes with a lower horizontal line of three symbols. Some of these touch each other, and their radial grooves run down the rock into large natural horizontal cracks.

It is proposed that the first symbol to be carved is the largest to the upper left as its rings are complete, whereas the outer rings of the next symbol to the right are squashed up against the left symbol, perhaps suggesting that the carver didn't allow for enough space for the carving. A carved line runs through the centres of the upper three symbols and, to the north-west, their radial grooves are aligned towards the setting midsummer sun as shown about 8.00pm on 20 June 1995. To the north-east, the symbols are aligned in the direction of the rising moon during a major standstill, while to the south-west, they are aligned towards the setting midwinter sun. Perhaps these symbols represent and reflect rituals carried out as the midwinter and midsummer sun set on the horizon, Azi.300°. Alt. 9°. Decl. +24°.

THE UPPER CAIRNBAAN CUP AND RING MARKS TO THE NORTH-WEST
NR 8387 9106. LAT. 56° 3' 48" N. LONG. 5° 28' 24" W

The midsummer sun setting in line with the upper Cairnbaan cup and ring marks, at 8:00pm, 20 June 1995.

SOME OF THE LOWER CAIRNBAAN CUP AND RING MARKS

The lower symbols being lit by the setting midsummer sun on 20 June 1995.

THE NORTH-WEST HORIZON FROM THE LOWER CUP AND RING MARKS

The grooves of these cup and ring marks are aligned towards the setting midsummer sun, as shown about 8.00pm on 20 June 1995. Perhaps these symbols represent the actual rituals to the midsummer sun as it set on the horizon. Azi. 300°. Alt. 9°. Decl. +24°.

THE SOUTHERN TEMPLE WOOD STONE CIRCLE

The Temple Wood Stone Circles

The Temple Wood stone circle was partially excavated by J.H. Craw (Craw 1929: 130–1). During Jack Scott's excavations in the 1970s, the remains of a smaller timber and stone circle were also found a short distance to the north-east. At the centre of the northern circle is a large north-south aligned slab. Apparently, the wooden posts of the northern circle were being replaced with stones when this was abandoned in order to build the southern circle, and this is thought to have happened during the Neolithic period (Scott, J.G. 1989: 391). Stone 7 has some cup marks on its outer side, while Stone 9 has two connecting spirals on it lower inner and outward sides. Stone 11 is carved with faint concentric circles on its outer side. Stone 8 also has some cup marks on its outer side. The inside of the southern circle showed signs of burning, and four small burial cairns were built in and around it during the Bronze Age. Dr Alison Sheridan later dated these small burial cairns to about 1200 BC, after which the circle was converted into a large burial cairn. (Sheridan 2012: 180).

During Scott's excavations, Dr J.C. Orkney's survey of the southern circle suggested that it was a Professor Alexander Thom Class A egg type, (Thom, Thom, Burl, 1980 (RCAHMS, 1999). Dr Orkney informed Dougie in a letter, that small potato-shaped stones were found bedded upright in distinctly orange coloured clay at some of the radial points of the arcs forming the circle. When J.G. Scott's and Dr Orkney's plan of the southern Temple Wood stone circle was overlain on an aerial picture taken by Dougie of the circle, they matched perfectly. From the southern circle, Professor Thom surveyed the Nether Largie Stones in 1936, and found that its two southern stones

1977 EXCAVATION OF THE TEMPLE WOOD STONE CIRCLE, ARGYLL

A burial cist made of large slabs was placed near the centre of the circle, and this and a nearby small kerb cairn had aligned false portals on their south-east sides. Note the height of the circle stones and how they are connected by low stones.

REMAINS OF TWO OF THE SMALL BURIAL CAIRNS INSIDE THE CIRCLE

The central burial cist is generally aligned towards the midwinter sunset and the northern rising major standstill moon. Surveys showed that the false portals were aligned to the rising southern major standstill moon. The false portal of the north-east cairn contained cremated bone, and just in front of it there was a long squared stone that was found resting on some smaller stones. Although it is slightly to the side, this recumbent stone may have had a similar function to those found in front of the false portals at the Kintraw and Culcharron cairns.

DOUBLE SPIRAL ON STONE 9

On the outer and inner sides of the northern Stone 9, there are two joined spirals similar to those found in the midwinter aligned passage cairn of Newgrange in Ireland; they probably symbolise the midwinter and the midsummer sun.

were indicating the rising midwinter sun, while the centre stone indicated the southern minor standstill moonrise. After the stump of a standing stone was found 260 metres to the south-west of the southern circle in 1973 by Aubrey Burl, its survey by Jon Patrick showed that it had indicated the southern major standstill moon setting on Bellanoch Hill.

Surveys in the late 1980s confirmed those by Thom, and the long axis of the larger circle was found to be aligned towards the stump of Burl's standing stone and the setting moon on Bellanoch Hill. The two false portals of the internal burial cairns were found to be aligned towards the rising major standstill moon. It was also noticed at that time that the two circles to the south-west were in line with the setting midwinter sun, and north-east to where the northern major standstill moon rose above the village of Kilmartin. From the southern circle, photographs were taken of the midwinter sun rising above the southern Nether Largie stones in 2001. The midwinter sun was photographed setting in line with the two circles in 2007.

STONE 11

On the outer right side of Stone 11 there is a faint symbol formed by two concentric circles.

SOUTH-WEST VIEW FROM THE CIRCLE TO BELLANOCH HILL

The circle's long axis passes through the two circles stones, 10 and 2, to the left of the picture, which are in line with the former position of S7, but this sightline is now blocked by the large tree. Jon Patrick's survey showed that S7, which was located just to the tree's right, indicated where the southern major standstill moon set behind Bellanoch Hill. This photograph was taken from between Stones 10 and 9 to show the sightline to Bellanoch Hill. The double spiral is located on the lower left of Stone 9.

NORTHERN TEMPLE WOOD STONE CIRCLE FROM THE SOUTH

Although there was no trace of burials in the northern circle, its excavation revealed that a ring of postholes once surrounded a central slab, which was thought to be aligned south towards the midday midwinter sun.

VIEW FROM THE SOUTHERN CIRCLE TO THE SOUTH-EAST NETHER LARGIE STANDING STONES

From the southern circle, Professor Thom's survey suggesting that the midwinter sun would have risen above the two southern Nether Largie stones (Thom 1967: 97. A 2/8). This was confirmed by the above photograph taken at 9.25am on 11 December 2001, Azi.140° 30'. Alt.1° 58'. Decl. -23° 55'. The Nether Largie stones cannot be seen in this photograph as they are still in the shadow of the hill, but Thom's survey suggesting that the central stone generally indicated the rising southern moon during its minor standstill, was confirmed by the 1992 surveys (Scott, D. 2012).

SIGHTLINE FROM THE NORTHERN TO THE SOUTHERN STONE CIRCLE

From the northern circle, the midwinter sun set above the southern circle at 3.28pm on 17 December 2007. Perhaps the double spirals and the concentric circles on Stones 10 and 12 depict the midwinter sunset. From the southern circle, shortly after the midwinter sun sets, the northern full moon will rise above the northern circle during a major standstill every 19–20 years. This sequence suggests that these circles were initially built to mark the setting midwinter sun and the rising northern major standstill moon. This is in keeping with later use of the Nether Largie stones.

THE CENTRAL AND NORTHERN NETHER LARGIE STONES
NR 82 97. LAT. 56° 7' 18" N. LONG. 5° 29' 43" W

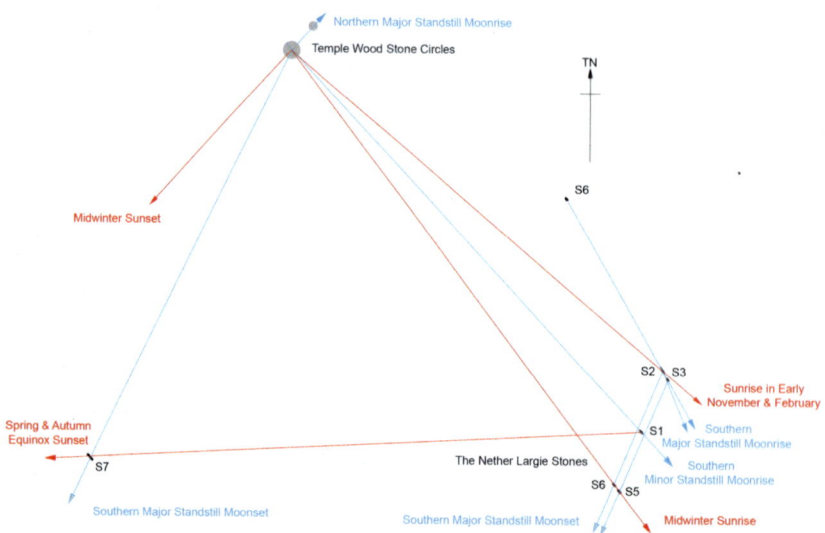

PLAN OF THE POSITIONS OF THE NETHER LARGIE STONES IN KILMARTIN, ARGYLL

This illustration shows the layout and the solar/lunar orientations between the Temple Wood stone circles and the Nether Largie standing stones in red and blue respectively. The stones are numbered after Thom (Thom 1971: 46–47). Thom suggested the southern and central stones were aligned to the north-west to where he thought the upper and lower edges of the northern major standstill moon set in a small horizon notch to the upper left of the Temple Wood circle. Ruggles showed that the southern stones were aligned to the north of the notch. Star trail photographs taken in 2001 from the central stone, showed that the northern moon would have set to the south of Thom's notch. Thom's surveys from the Southern Temple Wood circle suggest that the southern and central stones were marking the midwinter sunrise and the minor standstill moonrise (Thom, 1967: 97, Table 8.1). Surveys in 1989 and observations in 2006–7 confirmed that the midwinter sun and the southern major standstill moon would rise and set in line with these stones. From the central Nether Largie stone, the position of the stump of S7 was found to be marking the setting equinox sun. This sightline passes through the west gable end of the Poltalloch gatehouse.

The Nether Largie Stones

The Nether Largie Stones are located 500 metres to the south-east of the Temple Wood stone circles, about a kilometre south of Kilmartin. The layout of these stones is the most intriguing and sophisticated of all the standing stones Dougie has come across in Scotland. They are formed by two pairs of standing stones which are each placed to the south-west and north-east of a central standing stone. About 120 metres north-west of the two northern stones, there is an outlying standing stone. All these standing stones are aligned to the north-west and south-east. Just to the south of the central stone is a square setting of four small stones. The stump of another standing stone, S7, was found 300 metres to the west and was excavated by Aubrey Burl in 1973 (Hawkins 1973, 1983: 98, 100–2). With the exception of the latter stone and south-west

SOUTH-WEST ORIENTATION OF THE NETHER LARGIE STONES TOWARDS BELLANOCH HILL

As, looking south-west, the horizon is hidden by trees from the stones, Dougie climbed to the top of a high tree to see how they were aligned towards Bellanoch Hill. This showed that Thom's three stones were generally in line with the notch on Bellanoch Hill. However, the 1992 surveys showed that it was the four stones that marked where the moon set on the flatter horizon to the left of Bellanoch hill at this time.

stone, all five of the other stones are cup marked. The southern side of the central stone is also carved with a number of cup and ring marks.

When Professor Alexander Thom surveyed these stones in 1936, he suggested they indicated where the upper and lower edges of the extreme southern and northern major standstill moon set, with a high degree of accuracy in small notches on the south-west and west horizon. He also found the northern and southern stones were aligned to the rising southern moon and the midwinter sunrise. For some reason, he chose to ignore these indicated events and instead concentrated on his theory that the upper and lower edges of the moon set in the small notch above the Temple Wood stone circle. Thom also proposed that, diagonally from the two northern stones, the southern stones indicated where the extreme southern major standstill full moon would set in notches on Bellanoch Hill every 18.61 years.

Surveys in the late 1980s were found to be approximately the same as those found by Thom, Patrick and Ruggles. When Dougie surveyed the position of the standing stone stump, s7, from the central Nether Largie stone, it was found to have marked the setting sun at the equinoxes. Although we have to be careful about reading too much into our highly accurate theodolite surveys, the solar/lunar orientations of these stones go far beyond the needs of any simple burial monument.

THE NETHER LARGIE STONES FROM THE NORTH-EAST TO THE SOUTH-WEST

The moon is not always at its extreme southern position as it rises or sets and any small movement would have been impossible to see. From between the two northern stones, the southern moon would set behind the central cup marked stone. The moon could also have been watched from this stone as it set between the two southern stones over the course of three nights.

LOOKING SOUTH-EAST TOWARDS THE TWO NORTHERN AND CENTRAL STONES FROM THE NORTH-WEST OUTLYING STANDING STONE

The moon will rise in line with the two northern stones a few nights before reaching its southern major standstill position; perhaps this is what the three cup marks on its upper northern side represent. The height of the horizon was surveyed when the trees were cleared in the early 1990s, Azi.149° 20'. Alt. 2° 8'. Decl. -27° 00'. The north-west outlying stone used to be aligned toward the two northern standing stones, but over the years it twisted slightly in its socket as its angle gradually increased, finally falling in 2012. After it was excavated by Kilmartin House Museum, the stone was re-erected, but it was realigned in the wrong direction towards the two southern stones.

THE RISING MOON FROM THE NORTH-WEST OUTLIER

On 11 June 2006, Dougie had gone to the north-west outlier to see if the southern moon with a declination of -29° would have risen in line with the centre stone, as proposed by Jon Patrick (Hawkins 1983:100). The Nether Largie stones could not be seen in the total darkness, but this time lapsed photograph confirmed that the moon would have risen closer in line with the two northern stones a day or so earlier. This could have been used to give an early warning that the moon was close to its furthest south position.

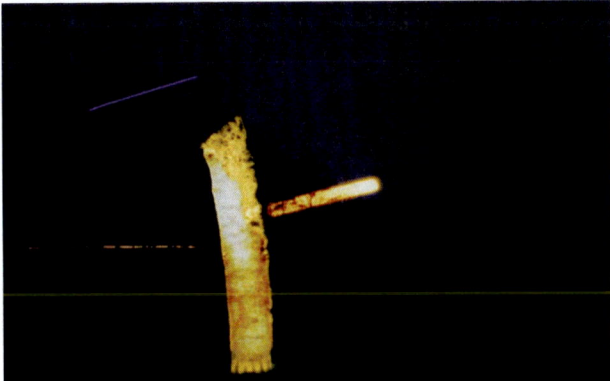

THE SOUTHERN MOON RISING IN LINE WITH THE TWO NORTHERN STONES

Dougie returned to the Nether Largie stones on 5 May 2007, and at around 12.13am, he was taken by surprise as the full moon, like a dull red ember, rose directly in line with the two northern stones, Azi. 153°. Alt. 1° 40'. Decl. -28°14'. A few hours later, as the moon began to set towards the two southern stones, it faded away and it was impossible to see in the bright misty pre-dawn light.

SHOWING HOW THE SOUTHERN MOON WILL RISE IN LINE WITH NORTHERN STONES AND THEN SET IN LINE WITH THE SOUTH-WEST STONES

This digitised image shows how, after rising in line with the two northern stones, the moon will then set in line with the three southern stones. Although the moon in its first crescent phase can be seen to set in line with the south-west stones in the winter, it would be difficult to see it rise in line with the two northern stones in this phase, as its light would washed out by the light of the sun, which is still high in the sky at this point.

THE SOUTHERN MOON SETTING BETWEEN THE TWO STANDING STONES TO THE SOUTH-WEST

As the sky began to clear at around 7.30pm on 29 September 2006, Dougie watched from the centre stone as the moon, with a declination of -29° 37' 25", set between the two southern Nether Largie stones. There is no evidence that these stones were used for the dead, and we must be careful about reading too much into their solar/lunar use until they can be archaeological excavated. As solar/lunar aligned burial monuments had been built for over 3,500 years, perhaps by 1200 BC their accumulated knowledge allowed these Bronze Age people to align these stones to something that we would recognise as astronomy.

THE MIDWINTER SUN RISING IN LINE WITH THE TWO SOUTHERN STANDING STONES

This photograph, taken shortly after the sun rose at 9.28am on 17 December 2007, verifies that the two leaning southern stones were originally aligned towards the rising sun near the winter solstice, Azi. 141° 38'. Alt. 2°47'. Decl. -23° 21'. Originally the winter solstice sun would have risen further down the slope to the right. Professor Thom shows from the southern Temple Wood circle that the Nether Largie stones were aligned to the rising major or minor standstill moon, and the midwinter sun. However, he focused more on his theory about the notch above the Temple Wood stone circle.

THE SETTING EQUINOX SUN FROM THE CENTRAL CUP AND RING MARKED STONE

The setting autumn equinox sun at 5.56pm on 21 September 2002. From Stone 1, the former position of Stone 7 was in line with the southern side of the Poltalloch Estate gatehouse, above which the sun will set on the days of the equinoxes, Azi. 264° 00'. Alt. 4° 30'. Decl. +0° 24'. Although most of the solar/lunar aligned monuments were clearly used for burials, the complexity between the Temple Wood circles and Nether Largie stones suggests that they were used to 'observe' the rising and setting sun and moon, and that they could have been used to predict eclipses of the sun or moon. A similar degree of sophistication can also be seen at Stonehenge and Calanais, which suggests that a deeper knowledge of the movements of the sun and moon existed during the Bronze Age.

South-West Scotland

BALLOCHMYLE SOUTHERN WALL, AYRSHIRE
NS 512255. LAT. 55° 30' 04" N. 4° 21' 32" W

Ballochmyle, Ayrshire

A FEW KILOMETRES south-east of Mauchline, at the north-west end of a small glen, is one of the most magnificent examples of Bronze Age rock art in Scotland. Shortly after their discovery in 1986, the earth ramp was removed, revealing the lower carvings. The symbols are carved on two east facing 10-metre sections of red sandstone walls running roughly north–south. The symbols range from cup and ring marks, linear cup marks, rayed discs, snaking lines, spirals, crescent moon and, most unusually for the 'art' of this period, the carving of three deer. The rayed discs are the same as those found in Irish solar-aligned tombs and could depict the sun, while there is another symbol that might represent a comet. Some of the symbols on the lower southern wall look very like crucibles, or bronze flat axes, perhaps suggesting that metal was smelted nearby. It is true that the symbols can tell us very little about what they had been used for, but from evidence found at other sites, this is possibly a sacred site where rituals were timed by the sun or moon rising along the eastern horizon. The flat wall between the two walls is carved with three round symbols, one of which looks like a fiery sun; this wall is aligned towards where the sun rose during the Bronze Age. Many of the cup marks on these walls are laid out in horizontal lines, which could only have been carved over an unknown period of time. The two joined symbols to the upper right of the northern wall are similar to other double discs of the period and could be the forerunners of the Pictish double discs. These are likely to symbolise the midsummer and midwinter sun.

NORTHERN WALL, BALLOCHMYLE, AYRSHIRE

On the left side of the northern wall above there is a crescent moon, and two rayed 'sun' discs. The symbol to the centre-right, which has two curved lines emerging from its top, could depict a comet. Below the S symbol is a glyph, which might be a representation of a Bronze Age boat.

TORHOUSE STONE CIRCLE, GALLOWAY
NX 38255 56493. LAT. 54° 52' 37" N. LONG. 4° 32' 20" W

AERIAL VIEW OF TORHOUSE STONE CIRCLE.

This aerial picture shows that the simplest way to create the flattened shape of the circle is by drawing a large arc across its south-east side. The stones are placed in approximate opposite pairs, which generally align with the southern setting major standstill moon.
The midwinter sunlight highlights the remains of a possible cairn that perhaps covered central stones aligned to the midsummer sunrise and midwinter sunset.

Torhouse Stone Circle, Galloway

This circle of 19 granite stones, one of the best preserved monuments of its type in the country and described (Symson 1684) as being 'King Gauldus's Tomb', is located near some stone rows on a slight terrace in the fields to the north-east of the river Bladnock. About 21 metres wide, it is graded in height south-east towards the highest cup marked circle stone. Near its centre, there are two large stones placed on either side of a smaller stone and these are aligned to the north-east and south-west, with the latter stone having fallen. They stand within what might be the remains of a cairn, where some bone was apparently found.

Torhouse Stone Circle has previously been described and planned by archaeologists (Coles 1897, Curl 1911 and Burl 1971, 1979). Burl compared the central stone setting with the recumbent stone circles of the north-east of Scotland and those in south-west Ireland (Burl). He also claimed that the flattened facades of the Cambret moor, Castle Rigg circles and some of the recumbent stones circles and Clava cairns in the north-east of Scotland, had been built in a similar way. From their surveys, many of these circles have been found to be solar or lunar aligned.

Although Dougie respects Professor Thom, he learned from experience to be wary of his proposed geometrically shaped circles. But when he looked at an aerial photograph he had taken of Torhouse, it seemed at first it was a Thom Type B circle. However, it was possible to create this shape by scribing a large arc across the south-east side of Torhouse from the end of the north-west axis. This technique also worked on Dougie's aerial photographs of other north-east monuments. Perhaps Thom was too focused on his complex Pythagorean geometry idea, and did not consider this simple way to explain the shape of these monuments (1976; 406, 211–2, 365).

Dougie's 1989 survey and observations on 8 November 2014 show that the sun will rise above the highest stone in early November and February. The axis line to the north-west marks the sunset in early May and August. The three central stones are aligned towards the midsummer sunrise and the midwinter sunset. Thom proposed that Torhouse was created with Pythagorean geometry and that it was a flattened Type A circle (Thom 1967, G 3/7; 137). The sunset photographed on 28 December 2003 (Scott 2016) shows that the circle's south-west axis aligns on the setting southern moon during a major standstill. It is very difficult to see the setting full moon in the bright summer morning light, so perhaps the shape of the circle is reflecting that of a gibbous moon as it sets earlier in a darker sky.

CUP MARKS ON THE HIGHEST CIRCLE STONE AT TORHOUSE, GALLOWAY

The highest circle stone has a large cup mark on its northern side, and there are also two artificial dimples on its lower inner side.

THE THREE CENTRAL STONES TO THE SOUTH-WEST

The three central stones originally aligned with the midwinter sunset, Azi. 227°. Alt. 1°. Decl. -22° 36'. This picture was taken at about 3.20pm on 28 December 2003, before the sun actually set, to allow time to get to drive to the Drumtroddan standing stones to photograph the midwinter sunset. The three stones at the centre of the circle are aligned to the north-east to the midsummer sunrise, Azi. 47°. Alt. 2°. Decl. +24° 36'.

VIEW TO THE SOUTH-EAST FROM THE CENTRAL STONES

Shortly after rising at about 7.40am on 8 November 2014, the sun briefly appeared through the clouds above the highest cup marked stone. The small stone at the centre of the circle is the focus of the sun at different times and perhaps it covers the cremated remains of a powerful individual remembered as 'King Galdus'?

TORHOUSE STONE CIRCLE TO THE EAST

The function of the monument's shape is unknown as it would have been simpler to build and grade a true circle to the November and February sunrise. It would seem from the circle's low height that it was not 'astronomically' used, and the bone that was found suggests that it was a solar-aligned burial monument. However, before any building began, someone must have watched and then geometrically set out the circle towards the sun at the times described.

THE THREE EASTERN STONES TO THE SOUTH-WEST
NX 38370 56500 LAT. 54° 52' 37" N LONG. 4° 31' 15" W

The three stones near the circle on the other side of the road are aligned towards the setting midwinter sun, as shown at 3.34pm on 16 December 2017, Azi. 222°. Alt. 1°. Decl. -24°. In the opposite direction, the stones are also aligned north-east to where the northern midwinter full moon will rise over the mountain of Cairnsmore of Fleet during a major standstill every 19–20 years, Azi. 40°. Alt. 2°. Decl. +28°.

THE MIDWINTER SUNRISE FROM CAULDSIDE BURN SPIRALLED BOULDER
NX 38370 56500 LAT. 54° 52' 37" N LONG.4° 31' 15" W

Cauldside Burn Linear Cemetery

On the lower southern slopes of Cambret Hill in Galloway, there is a large slab which is carved with one of the most remarkable pieces of rock art in Scotland. This comprises a worn grooved cup mark from which a large six-ring clockwise spiral connects to a smaller spiral or cup and ring mark. Below this, there is also a long straight groove that connects to a faint cup and ring mark at its south-west end. A short distance to the north-west of the spiral stone there is a large boulder that has been split by a line of drill holes. About 100 metres to the north-east, there is a possible leaning standing stone. This intriguing rock carving is located at the north-west end of a line of four other Bronze Age monuments, which are strung out across the valley towards the hill of Cairnharrow (Coles 1898: 368–9). The first of these is the remains of a 13-metre-wide burial cairn, which was followed by an alignment of two standing

CAULDSIDE BURN DOUBLE-SPIRALLED BOULDER TO THE NORTH

SHOWING THE DETAILS OF THE CARVING ON THE BOULDER AT CAULDSIDE BURN

A line drawn between three of the cup marks on this stone generally aligns with the midsummer sunrise and the midwinter sunset. To the north-east, the sun will generally rise in line with the spiral stone at midsummer. The possible leaning standing stone indicates the sunrise in early May and August, which equates with the later Gaelic festivals of Beltane and Lughnasad, some 45 days before and after midsummer.

stones that are no longer visible. This is followed by a large burial cairn and a 30-metre-wide circle of low standing stones. To find the spiralled boulder, go straight down the hill from the Cambret Hill transmitter, following the east side of a long narrow band of ferns while lining up the large burial cairn with the top right side of Cairnharrow.

Professor Thom did not mention the spiralled boulder, but his survey from the north-east cairn showed that these five monuments were aligned to the midwinter sunrise (Thom, 1967, Cauldside, G 4/14: 59 Fig. 6.3). From the spiralled boulder, a survey also found that these cairns were aligned to the midwinter sun rising from behind the hill of Cairnharrow, Azi.160°. Alt. 9° 44'. Decl. -23°. The double spiral is skewed to the line of monuments

and is aligned towards the midsummer sunrise and the midwinter sunset. The possible north-east standing stone indicates the sunrise in early May and August, some 45 days before and after midsummer. Midwinter-aligned spirals can be seen at Eggerness in Galloway and the Long Meg standing stone in Cumbria, and from the northern Temple Wood stone circle in Argyll (Scott, D. 2016: 45–66). The spirals on the Achnabreck rock outcrop in Argyll are aligned towards the midsummer sunset and midwinter sunrise. On 15 December 2017, the midwinter sun was photographed rising from behind Cairnharrow, and a few hours later the sun set in line with the double spiral. It is likely that the double spiral was ritually carved to venerate the path of the sun from midwinter to midsummer. This shows that they were able

THE CAULDSIDE SPIRALLED BOULDER TO THE SOUTH-WEST

The setting midwinter sun was seen from the spiralled rock for the first time in 4,000 years, at 3.41pm on 15 December 2018. This outstanding example of rock art confirms its connection with the midwinter and midsummer sun. It would seem from the similar solar-aligned symbols on the other monuments described, that they were religious expressions to the sun as it rose out of, or set into, the underworld of the spirit ancestors.

to conceptualise the sun setting into and rising from under the earth throughout the year. The idea that spirals and cup and ring marks symbolise the sun is best exemplified by those carved on the midwinter aligned tomb of Newgrange in Ireland.

After 4,000 years of exposure to the elements, the carvings are very faint, and they are easier to see in low winter light or when wet. There are also a few faint cup marks within the lower rings of the spiral, which is also cut by two radial groves. The upper radial groove, like many of these symbols, appears to be pushing through the spiral rings. From the spiral stone, the four other monuments are aligned south-east to where the rising midwinter sun appears from behind the top of Cairnharrow. On 15 December, the top of the hill was covered with cloud and by the time it cleared, the sun had moved out of line with the monuments.

At Drumtroddan farm, the main concentration of the symbols is on three flat panels of bedrock (see pictures overleaf). Some of these are in rows along the top of the north-west edge of the largest triangular panel, perhaps suggesting they were the first symbols to be carved. The radial groove of the symbol to the left aligns with the midsummer sunset and, while those to the right might also be reflecting this event, they might represent the setting northern midwinter major standstill full moon. In the opposite direction, some of the grooves point towards the midwinter sunrise.

THE DRUMTRODDAN 1 CUP AND RING MARKS TO THE NORTH-WEST
NX 363447 LAT. 54° 46' 14" N. LONG. 4° 32' 48" W

At Drumtroddan Farm the two carved areas of bedrock are called Drumtroddan 1, 2, which are located some 28 metres to the north-west and south-east of each other. Most of the Drumtroddan 1 symbols are joined by grooves forming double rings, which are aligned in both directions towards the midsummer sunset, and the midwinter sun rising above the cup and ring marks of Drumtroddan 2.

THE CUP AND RING MARKS TO THE SOUTH-WEST

The large cup and ring mark on the detached block is joined by grooves to three smaller south-east symbols. The lines of symbols to the south-west and north-east are aligned towards the setting midwinter sun and the rising midsummer sun.

THE CUP AND RING MARKS ON THE DETACHED BLOCK TO THE SOUTH-EAST

This picture shows the sun generally rising in line with the joined cup and ring marks at 8.56am on 15 December 2017. During the Neolithic Period, the sun would have risen in line with the large right cup and ring mark within Drumtroddan 2, near the winter solstice. The smaller cup and ring marks to the left of the centre groove could represent the midwinter sun rising along the horizon towards its winter solstice position. The symbols to the right could symbolise moon as it moves south to where it will rise on the top of the hill at its southern major standstill. This moonrise was indicated by the three Drumtroddan stones some 477 metres away, but only one of these stones is now standing.

MIDWINTER SUNRISE FROM DRUMTRODDAN 2

The midwinter sun rising in line with the groove of one of the large cup and ring marked stones within Drumtroddan 2 on 15 December 2017. Perhaps making the symbol was part of sacred rituals venerating and celebrating the rebirth of the midwinter sun as it rose out of the Underworld.

DRUMTRODDEN STANDING STONES TO THE NORTH-EAST

These three standing stones were originally aligned north-east towards the midsummer sunrise, Azi. 44°. Alt. 0° 30'. Decl. +24°. Like many other stone rows, it's possible that these stones formed a solar-aligned burial monument. There is a large cup mark on the west side of the south-east stone, but this is now hidden on its underside, as it fell sometime after 2004, meaning that its alignment to the midsummer sunrise could not be photographed. This was reported to RCAHMS. As far as we are aware, its socket was not excavated, which is unfortunate as it could have established if the stones were used to mark burials.

DRUMTRODDEN STANDING STONES TO THE SOUTH-WEST

To the south-west the stones were aligned to the midwinter sun setting into the sea some 4,000 years ago, Azi. 224°. Alt. 0° 20'. Decl. -24°. The setting midwinter sun at about 3.45pm on 28 December 2003.

Re-use of Monuments in the Pictish Period

THE WHITEBRIDGE LINEAR PICTISH CEMETERY, HIGHLAND
NH 49275 17113 LAT. 57° 13' 12" N LONG. 4° 29' 52" W

Part of the Pictish linear cemetery at Whitebridge, which, as shown at 10.38am on 27 December 2016, is aligned towards the rising midwinter sun.

Continuity of the Sun

AT THE END of the Bronze Age, there seems to have been a climatic change to colder and wetter conditions, which led to the abandonment of settlements and monuments on the higher ground. It was around this time that hilltops were turned into fortresses and there was an increase in making weapons. From the gold and swords found deposited in lakes, rivers and bogs, it would appear that some of the beliefs changed to the worship of water gods. This change in the weather is thought to have halted the building of stone circles and cairns. Dougie's research had suggested a solar/lunar continuity from the Neolithic, through the Bronze and Iron Age to the Pictish period (Scott, D. 2004). It was thought that the Clava cairns near Inverness were Neolithic, but these have been dated to the early Bronze Age (Bradley 2000). Bradley found that a small cup marked kerb cairn, located a short distance to the west of the central ring cairn, had been built a thousand years after the other cairns. When surveyed, this small cairn was found to be graded in height towards the midwinter sunset and the cup marked kerbstone to the rising sun at the equinoxes.

The Laikenbuie ring cairn was excavated from 2003–6 and it was dated to about 600 AD in the Iron Age (Bradley 2016). Dougie's 2008 survey found that this cairn was graded in height to the south-south-east to where the southern moon rises during a major standstill moon every 19–20 years. The Bronze Age recumbent stone circles are also orientated to the sun and moon. The solar/lunar continuity can also be seen in the abstract images of the solar chariot on Roman and Iceni coins from southern Britain and this could only have been derived from commonly held beliefs. The idea that the cup marks are linked to the ancestors also fits with the concept that the Pictish double disc symbols and Z-rod are family or tribal emblems. In *The Golden Bough*, James George Frazer describes 18th century accounts of how fire festivals, such as Beltane in May and Samhain in November, occurred throughout the Highlands to protect people and animals against disease, to encourage fertility and ward off evil (by burning witch effigies as ritual sacrifices to the sun god, Bel). These festivals took place every 45 days and included fires at midwinter as well as midsummer. Frazer also mentions that 'bonfire' is derived from 'bone-fire' and gives examples of how bone should be burnt in order to bring good luck and drive off witches or other evil influences that might poison the water or the land.

This tradition could be linked back to the ritual cremations of bones during the Bronze Age, 4,000 years ago. Frazer also describes how bonfires were lit on round green hillocks called Cnoc or Tom-nan-ainnel ('hill of the fires'). He describes one of these mounds at Killin in Perthshire as being surrounded by the remains of a wall with a small standing stone on its top (Frazer 1914). It is likely that this is a burial cairn, the earth from which was thought to have curative power when rubbed on the affected part of a diseased animal. As some Bronze Age alignments are carved with Pictish symbols, it seems obvious that the Picts also celebrated these festivals. The Class 1 symbols have been dated from the 3rd century AD onward, with the Class 2, from about the 8th century, showing the obvious influence of the Irish Celtic Church. The Class 1 style is found in different combinations of animal and geometric forms on prehistoric standing stones and has been found in association with burials at Garbeg and Dunrobin and at Tilytarmont. An early Pictish symbol was found in a Shetland broch lying below a layer dated to the 4th century AD (Ritchie, G. *pers comms*). As the symbols appear fully formed on the stones with no evidence of prototypes, it is possible that they were painted on wood long before they were carved on the stones. It is generally accepted that they are tribal symbols, perhaps representing political marriages to strengthen alliances against the threat of a common invader.

Pictish Stones

The Craw Stane near Rhynie in Aberdeenshire has two Class 1 symbols, one of a leaping salmon and another of the Pictish beast on its southern side. The Craw Stane (Crow Stone) near Rhynie in Aberdeenshire had fallen but was re-erected in the late 19th century; it is carved with a salmon leaping over a Pictish Beast symbol. Gordon Noble's excavations have found that the Craw Stane had stood next to the entrance of a possible Pictish Royal Palace. To the south-east of the Craw Stane, a large hole was excavated which is the possible position of the Rhynie Man Stone, which is carved with a fierce warrior carrying a large axe. It is possible that these

SOME OF THE JOINED CUP AND RING MARKS ON THE NORTHERN BALLOCHMYLE WALL
NS 512255. LAT. 55° 30' 04" N. 4° 21' 32" W

These connected Bronze Age disc symbols on the north Ballochmyle wall could have been the inspiration for the later Pictish Double-Discs.

Pictish symbols were carved on solar-aligned Bronze Age standing stones.

During the 19th century, a stone with a Pictish beast arcing over a crescent and V-rod was relocated within the circle henge at Crichie near Inverurie (Ritchie 1919–20: 17). Ritchie's map shows that the stone was originally located to the north-east of the circle, which is where the sun rises in early May and August. Like many others, this stone was possibly reused by the Picts, similar to those found near recumbent stone circles at Brandsbutt and Kirkton of Bourtie. Fred Coles suggested that the two Nether Corskie stones near Dunecht were the remains of a recumbent stone circle (Coles: 83–4). Adam Welfare has proposed that these two stones actually formed an east-west alignment (Welfare 2011: 16). On the west stone, there are two cup marks as well as Pictish mirror case and mirror and comb symbols (Ritchie 1914–5: 34–9).

If the Nether Corskie stones were the remains of a recumbent stone circle, from an approximate centre, the southern moon would have set in line with its recumbent stone, while the midwinter sun would have set behind the Pictish symbol stone. It is also possible that these flanking stones were aligned to the rising and setting sun near the equinoxes in the same way as the flankers of the Sunhoney circle are aligned to the midwinter sunrise and midsummer sunset. However, to prove this would require further surveys and excavations. As the Pictish mirror case has crescents, it is suggested that it is actually half a solar/lunar double disc symbol. Along with the cup marks, this would suggest that these stones were used for over 3,500 years to mark the rising and setting sun at the equinoxes and at midwinter. It is generally thought that the mirror case symbol represents a container for a mirror. However, as the squared section of these mirror case symbols are sometimes depicted with crescents, it is in effect a double disc with one of the discs removed and its position on the Nether Corskie stone could suggest it represents the midwinter sun. If so, this means the Picts knew that

THE NETHER CORSKIE STANDING STONES, GRAMPIAN
NJ74829 09599 LAT. 57° 10' 36" N LONG. 2° 25' 05" W

These two stones and the large stone lying between them are thought to be the remains of a recumbent stone circle, but it has been proposed that they are in fact a simple alignment of standing stones (Welfare, 2011, p16). The west stone, shown here to the left, is a rough, red, hard granite and is carved with two cup marks and two class 1 Pictish symbols. This would have been difficult to carve, and why it was chosen for the Pictish symbols is unknown, as the other smoother stone would have been more suitable for this. This would suggest that the Pictish symbols were linked in some way with the cup marks.

THE PICTISH SYMBOLS AND CUP MARK ON THE WEST STONE AT NETHER CORSKIE

One of the cup marks can be seen to the left of the two Pictish symbols comprising a mirror and comb and the so-called mirror case. However, as the lower part of the latter symbol is carved with lunar crescents, it is in fact half a Double-Disc symbol. The other cup mark is on the left side of the stone. The possible recumbent and the cup mark on the western side of the Pictish symbol stone. To the east and west the sun will rise and set in line with these stones at the spring and the autumn equinoxes. If, as seen at the solar-aligned Edderton and Aberlemno stones, that the Double-Disc could symbolises the midsummer and midwinter sun, does the use of half a Double-Disc on this stone represents the halfway point of the year at the equinoxes?

THE NETHER CORSKIE STANDING STONES TO THE SOUTH-WEST

If these stones are the remains of a recumbent stone circle, from its centre the southern major standstill moon would have set in line with the recumbent every 19–20 years, Azi. 195°. Alt. 2° 30'. Decl. -29°. The midwinter sun also set behind the Pictish symbol stone at about 2:45pm on 19 December 2002, Azi. 212°. Alt. 3°. Decl. -24°.

the stone and the cup marks were somehow connected with this event. The Class 1 symbols are found on Bronze Age standing stones, some of which are also cup marked. Apart from the Edderton stone, there are three other solar-aligned Pictish symbol stones.

At Aberlemno in Angus, there are two stones standing next to the main road about 30 metres north-east to the south-west of each other. The north-east stone has the Pictish symbols of a serpent above a large Pictish double disc next to a mirror and comb on its north side; on its other side, there are six large cup marks. The south-west stone is cup marked and also has the remains of different sized Pictish circles carved on its northern side. The alignment works in two directions. From the north-east Pictish symbol stone, the Crescent Stone points to where the midwinter sun would have set 4,000 years ago. In the opposite direction the midwinter full moon would have risen every 19–20 years. The other alignments are at Peterhead Farm near Blackford in Perthshire and near the Ardlair recumbent stone circle in Aberdeenshire. The two stones at Ardlair are located about 300 metres away to the north-east from the recumbent stone circle and they could have formed a separate monument. The two stones are about 20 metres apart, with the stone nearest the circle having Pictish Class 1 symbols of the Pictish beast, split sword and mirror on its south side. From the circle, these stones point to where the sun rises near the times of the festivals of Samhain and Bride in early November and February. The first time Dougie visited Ardlair on 4 May 1992, as he saw the sun set in line with the stones and the circle, he knew that they were marking the ancient festivals of Beltane and Lughnasad.

ARDLAIR STANDING STONES TO THE NORTH-WEST
NJ 55269 27940 LAT. 57° 20' 23" N LONG. 2° 44' 41" W

These two stones are in line with the ruined Ardlair recumbent stone circle on the hill to the north-west and the area is dominated by the great hill fort of Tap O' Noth. There are two long cup marked stones placed at right angles to the inner side of the recumbent stone and these are thought to have symbolised a passage into the circle, and this is in line with the rising southern major standstill moon every 19–20 years. From the circle, there is a fallen, cup marked standing stone lying a short distance down the slope. This is roughly in line with the other two stones, some 300 metres to the north-east. Thom's surveys suggest that these stones marked the rising sun in early November and February (Thom 1967: 98 Table 8.3. B 1/18).

PICTISH SYMBOLS ON THE INNER SIDE OF THE WEST STONE

The pointed stone is carved on its inner side by three faint Class I Pictish symbols of a Pictish Beast, a split sword, and a mirror and comb, but these do not have any obvious "astronomical" symbolism.

ARDLAIR STANDING STONES AT THE SETTING OF THE BELTANE SUN, 1992

On his first visit to Ardlair on 6 May 1992, Dougie saw the Beltane sun set directly in line with the stone circle, and he knew that this would occur again in early August at Lughnasad. This higher quality picture was taken at 7.33pm on 5 May 2018, Azi. 297°. Alt. 2° 30'. Decl. +16°. These times happen some 45 days before and after midsummer. One of the most interesting aspects of these stones is that they are marking where the sun rises out of and sets into what appear to be feminine shaped hills at the four sacred times of the year, and this could have been believed as a solar rebirth and the impregnation of the Earth by the sun.

ARDLAIR STANDING STONES TO THE SOUTH-EAST

The view to the south-east, where the sun will appear to rise out of Bennachie at Samhain in early November and Imbolc in early February, some 45 days before and after midwinter. The breast-shape top of Bennachie is also known locally as the Mither Tap (Mother's Pap?) as from most of the surrounding country side it looks like a woman lying on her back. A local ancient legend tells of how the giants of Tap O' Noth and Bennachie would throw large stones at each other, and this and their pap names could suggest that these were believed to be female giants.

Although further research is required, surveys of the Whitebridge, Garbeg and Tarradale Pictish linear barrow cemeteries near Inverness have shown that they are 'aligned' in the general directions of some of the eight divisions of the year. These are similar to the direction of the Neolithic and Bronze Age solar/lunar-aligned linear cemeteries of the Kilmartin Glen and the Clava cairns. The entrances of a large number of Brochs are also aligned to these times. Although at these last three solar-orientated sites there is no solar aspect to the Pictish symbols, the same cannot be said for the double discs at Edderton and Aberlemno and the single disc from Nether Corskie. These few examples show there were probably other Pictish Class 1 symbols on alignments that have been destroyed without their position being recorded. This has continued over the last 150 years by the removal of many Pictish standing stones from their original positions in order to preserve them. But doing so destroys the very evidence that helps us understand what the stones were originally used for.

Sun Discs

Continuity between the Bronze Age and Pictish period can be seen in a number of other moved Pictish cup marked stones. One in Dingwall parish churchyard has cup marks and Pictish symbols on both sides. These consist of a Crescent and V-rod below three circles in a triangular pattern and, on the other side, there is a double disc placed above a Crescent and V-rod. At Banchory House near Aberdeen, there is another double disc symbol stone with cup marks (Ritchie 1914–15: 33–49). A slab from a burial cist from Roseisle is carved with a Pictish salmon and a goose which has two cup marks at its centre. The Pictish Christian cross-slab at Glamis has, on its reverse side, a serpent, salmon and a mirror symbol. A cup mark can be seen at the centre of the salmon and others have been found near its base.

Out of the 40 Class 1 double discs, only two resemble the sun in the form of simple spirals or rayed discs, as on the Dunnichen and Alyth stones in Angus and Perthshire. A rayed disc can be found above two Pictish crescent and V-rod symbols on a stone built into the church wall at Knockando in Nairnshire. Outside Tain Museum in Easter Ross, there is a large stone from Ardjachie, with a rayed disc surrounded by cup marks. This disc is 'joined' to the lower of two circles of seven cup marks by a single cup mark

ARDJACHIE CUP MARKED PICTISH SYMBOL STONE, TAIN MUSEUM
NH 78025 82132 LAT. 57° 48' 44" N LONG. 4° 03' 17" W

and there is also an L-shaped Pictish symbol on the stone. A similar symbol was found along with a Crescent and V-rod, and mirror and comb on a Pictish stone from Ardross in Easter Ross, which is now in Inverness Museum along with other Pictish stones.

On the Ardjachie Stone, there is a faint groove running through the centre of the sun disc at an angle, which then cuts back to the horizontal to connect with the L-shaped symbol. As there is an obvious relationship between the sun disc and the cup marks, it is possible this is an earlier form of a Pictish double disc and Z-rod.

In regard to the purpose of the early Pictish symbols, apart from a few metal artefacts, all we really have to go on are the stones themselves. Although their main concentration is on the east side of the country, nine Pictish symbol stones have been found on the west coast, such as those on the Dunadd and Trusty's hill forts in Argyll and in Galloway. Could these be part of a shared cultural inheritance? In the light of Campbell's suggestion (Campbell 2000) that the Scots of Dalriada were themselves indigenous to the area, with long-established links to Ulster, and the current thinking that sees the Scots and Picts as much more interrelated than was previously thought (Broun 2008), such an idea has much to recommend it. Recent suggestions of a 3rd century date for the earliest symbol stones (Noble 2018) would also tend to support this possibility.

If the symbols were ancestral totems, they could have been painted on leather or carved on wood for centuries, each one linked to some tribal mythology, and perhaps it was with the threat of an invader they began to appear on the stones. Given the accepted 6th–7th century dates, it was thought that the threat was from the Northumbrians, but if the symbol stones are older than previously thought, could the invaders have been the Romans? On the Collessie Pictish symbol stone in Fife, there is a naked warrior wearing a cloak and carrying a shield and a ball-ended spear. This corresponds directly with a description of indigenous warriors from Dio Cassio writing in 217 AD:

> They dwell in tents, naked and unshod... For arms they have a shield and a short spear, with a bronze apple attached to the end of the spear-shaft, so that when it is shaken it may clash and terrify the enemy; and they also have daggers.

A stone with the Pictish beast above a crescent and V-rod was relocated in the circle henge at Crichie sometime in the 19th century after some of its original stones were destroyed (os NJ 779196). A survey of its original position from Ritchie's map equated with the sunrise of the Gaelic festivals of Beltane and Lughnasad. In 83 AD, the main Roman thrust was up the east coast into the Caledonian heartland which, according to Tacitus, culminated in the Roman victory at the battle of Mons Graupius the following year, for which of course we have only one Roman record. Within a few years, there are signs that the northern Roman forts were abandoned and by the end of the century they had fallen back to the Tyne-Solway line. This would later form the course of Hadrian's Wall, built in 120 AD.

Over the next 100 years, the Romans made periodic thrusts back into the north. By 139 AD, they had constructed the Antonine Wall between the Forth and Clyde, which was only used for approximately

THE DUNNICHEN STONE, FORFAR MUSEUM, ANGUS

The best example that the Pictish Double-Disc and Z Rod is a solar/lunar symbol can be seen on the Dunnichen Stone, which is on display in the Forfar Museum in Angus.

20 years before it too was abandoned. In 208 AD, the Emperor Severus came all the way from Rome to campaign against the joint forces of Caledonii and the Maeatae. We have no reports of any more large battles and a reference from Dio Cassio that the indigenous warriors plunge into the swamps and exist there for many days with only their heads above water may suggest that resistance to Roman attempts at conquest was more guerrilla-like in nature than any attempt to meet the organised Roman killing machine in pitched battles. This would conform to the known practice of small-scale, inter-tribal cattle raiding, which appears to have begun at least as early as the Iron Age and lasted into the 18th century among the Highland clans. Once the Severan Army had retreated south, the Caledonii and the Maeatae were soon causing havoc along the frontier and the Romans thereafter stayed mainly south of Hadrian's Wall.

Is it possible that during those times of deep uncertainty, in the lulls between the Roman expansion and contractions, the native Caledonians decided to form a more cohesive force which was reflected in the symbols? Is this what we see in the alliance between the Caledonii, the Maeatae, and the rest of the tribes as suggested by Agricola, an alliance that apparently reappears in the late 4th century in what the Romans referred to as the Barbarian Conspiracy? While the Picts might not have been able to defeat the Romans in a head-to-head battle, did they give them a harder time than we think? Dio Cassio certainly suggests this when he wrote:

> Severus, accordingly, desiring to subjugate the whole of it, invaded Caledonia. But as he advanced through the country, he experienced countless hardships in cutting down the forests, leveling the heights, filling up the swamps, and bridging the rivers; but he fought no battle and beheld no enemy in battle array. The enemy purposefully put sheep and cattle in front of the soldiers for them to seize, in order that they might be lured on still further until they were worn out; for in fact the water caused great suffering to the Romans, and when they became scattered, they would be attacked. Then unable to walk, they would be slain by their own men, in order to avoid capture, so that a full 50,000 of them died. But Severus did not desist until he approached the extremity of the island… he returned to the friendly proportion, after he had forced the Britons to come to terms, on the condition that they should abandon a large part of their territory (1927: 6–7).

This last statement about abandoning a large part of their territory is directly contradicted by his army retreating back behind Hadrian's Wall, which had effectively marked the limit of the Roman Empire since the abandonment of the Antonine Wall half a century earlier. It is unclear, but is Dio suggesting that the Romans had lost 50,000 men fighting the northern tribes? If so, this might account for them staying behind Hadrian's Wall until it was overrun in the Barbarian Conspiracy of 360 AD. Roman silver found in the area of Pictland was generally thought to have been looted, but it has been proposed that these were Roman bribes to placate the local tribes. This was concluded as some of the silver was cut into standard Roman weights, and its burial by the Picts at the Norrie's Law cairn in Fife, Balbirnie in Moray and standing stone sites at Dairsie in Fife and Belledrum near Inverness, are thought to have been

votive offerings to their gods (Dr Fraser Hunter *pers comms*). Remote surveys suggested the Belladrum standing stones were aligned to the southern major standstill moon, while those at Dairsie to the midsummer sunset. This could mean that the sun and moon and the ancestor gods were still being revered at these monuments in the 4th century AD. This would also explain the Roman gold coins and Romano brooches found in front of the blocked entrance of Newgrange in Ireland (O'Kelly 1982: 59).

The Scots and the Picts were warrior societies which often identify with fierce animal totems and perhaps this explains the 'Pictish' boar at Dunadd. Pictish symbols stones have been found with burials, and they could have been used to identify the dead person's lineage within their tribal group. It may be worth considering whether this could have been the start of a traditional use of the symbols that were later to be depicted on the 8th or 9th century Christian cross-slabs. If this was so, it would suggest the earliest example of Pictish Class 1 symbols on the stones could be dated to around the first half of the 2nd century, but some, like the solar double disc, seem to be rooted in the Bronze Age.

Just as the evidence shows continuity of the use of solar alignments, so it is worth considering whether the symbols used on the stones reflect another type of continuity, for as we have seen, representational art had been used here in carvings on stone since much earlier times.

EGGERNESS DEER AND CUP MARKED STONE, GALLOWAY
NX 48619 47300 LAT. 54° 47' 52" N LONG. 4° 21' 23" W

A short distance from the Eggerness spiralled rock sheet there is a flat stone carved with three deer. The top one has an internal S spiral at the muscle joints like the Pictish Dores boar and the Burghead bull. Next to these are two cup marks.

ALYTH CHURCH PICTISH SYMBOL STONE
NO 24514 48840 LAT. 56° 37' 31" N LONG. 3° 13' 55" W

The surviving rayed 'Sun Disc' of the Class 1 Pictish Double-Disc and Zed Rod symbol on the Alyth Cross Slab.

KNOCKANDO CHURCH PICTISH SYMBOL STONE
NJ 18643 42881 LAT. 57° 28' 08" N LONG. 3° 21' 29" W

BRANDSBUTT PICTISH SYMBOL STONE
NJ 75992 22405 LAT. 57° 17' 30" N LONG. 2° 24' 00" W

The Pictish symbol stone at Brandsbutt near Inverurie was found next to a recumbent stone circle. NJ 760223.

CLACH BIORACH PICTISH SYMBOL STONE

The Pictish symbols of a salmon leaping over a Double-Disc and Z rod on the north side of the Clach Biorach. Research suggests that the Double-Discs symbolise the sun some six months apart and these are joined by lunar crescents depicting the first and last phase of the moon during the lunar month.

Edderton Stone Circle

On the southern side of the Dornoch Firth, just outside the village of Edderton, are the remains of a stone circle and a large 4-metre-high standing stone called the Clach Biorach (pointed stone) which is carved with Pictish Class 1 symbols and is located in the field to the south-west. This was shown to Dougie by his friend Iain Fraser, who was born in the village.

The circle was built in the Bronze Age but the accepted date for the two Class 1 Pictish symbols consisting of a salmon leaping above a double disc and Z-rod is about 300–600 AD, which is 2,500 thousand years after the circle and the stone were created.

The double disc symbol has two inner concentric circles with the lower disc having a smaller circle displaced to its top. This also had a small artificial hole to its top, which is the first of four holes running around the eastern side of the stone which finishes with a large deep hole at the centre of its southern side. Just above the last two holes is a faint horizontal line of what might be a form of writing called Ogam. It seems that the stone once stood at the centre of what could be the remains of a burial mound. While there is no trace of the mound today, Iain said that, according to local legend, the standing stone marked the burial site of a Viking leader who was killed in a battle against the Scots. This is a common piece of folklore found throughout the country to explain these sites. However, the source of this piece of oral history comes from the Statistical Accounts of 1791 and 1845 that states: 'as some skeletons had been unearthed near the circle, they were possibly burials resulting from a battle'. In 1866, the Reverend Joass excavated the circle and found the burial cist which contained a beaker packed with charcoal, burnt bone and a few teeth (Joass 1866: 268–9). The remains of this beaker are now in the museum at Dunrobin Castle.

Only the north-western half of the 13-metre-wide circle remains in the form of an arc of five stones with the burial cist at its centre, and there might be the remains of a wide encircling ditch on its northern side. The two stones forming the open end of the circle are directly in line with the standing stone and the hill of Tor Leathan some 11km away to the south-west. A survey and later observations showed that the sun would set on top of Tor Leathan in early November and February. It is likely that the Clach Biorach marking the November and February sunset was for the benefit of the spirit ancestor in the burial cist.

EDDERTON STONE CIRCLE
NH 709852. LAT. 57° 50' 12.83" N. LONG. 4°11' 33" W

EDDERTON STONE CIRCLE TO THE SOUTH-WEST

From the circle, the Clach Biorach points to where the sun will set around 4.23pm on 5 November and 4 February, Azi. 233°. Alt. 2° 48'. Decl. -16°. These times are known as a winter cross quarter dates, and they occur some 45 days before and after midwinter. These are the same times as the later Gaelic festivals of Samhain, Sowain and Bride. In other parts of the British Isles, the festival of Bride is known as Imbolc.

Rayed Discs, Cup Marks and Pictish Symbols

The rayed discs on the Ardjachie and Knockando stones are similar to those found in some solar-aligned Irish Neolithic passage cairns and on the northern Ballochmyle wall in Ayrshire. The rayed disc above two Pictish Crescent and V-Rods on the Knockando Stone in Strathspey are very faint and the original location of this stone is unknown. However, the rayed disc and cup marks on the Ardjachie Stone could be Neolithic or Bronze Age in date, with the L-shaped symbol dating to the early medieval period. The rayed disc in Alyth church is part of a Pictish solar/lunar Double-Disc, in Perthshire. Pictish Double-Discs and Crescent and V-rod symbols are also found on the cup marked stone in Dingwall, in Easter Ross. One of the two Nether Corskie stones in Aberdeenshire has half a Double-Disc and Mirror and Comb symbols on its southern side next to several cup marks. The two Pictish stones Aberlemno roadside in Angus are still in their original positions and the north-east stone has six cup marks on its lower east side. There are cup marks on the Pictish Deer Stone at Eggerness, in Galloway. The simple explanation for this is that the Picts were making connections through cup marks to the ancestors and with the sun and moon.

As the sun disc on the Ardjachie stone is surrounded by cup marks, it may well have been carved 4,000 years ago, and the right-angled symbol could have been carved by the Picts at around the 5th century AD. According to Professor Charles Thomas, the Pictish Double-Disc symbol evolved from Bronze Age cup and ring marks (Thomas 1963: 31–97). In Gaelic, cup marked stones were called Clach Aoraidh (the worship stones).

There are also a number of joined cup and ring marks on the northern Ballochmyle wall and on the buried Cochno stone near Glasgow that look like Pictish Double-Disc symbols. There is another carved on the Monzie cup and ring marked outlier in Perthshire. As mentioned in Part 1, the Sidhe were believed to be spirits that lived in cairns and standing stones and it's likely they are a faint cultural memory in the belief of the spirits of the people who were buried in Neolithic and Bronze Age cairns. Surveys of alignments of cup marked standing stones suggest this contact was made when the sun or moon rose or set in line with the stones at the eight divisions of the year.

Links to Christianity

The establishment of Christianity over the earlier beliefs of the Picts by the 8th century AD can be seen in the way the solar Pictish double disc symbol was merged with Irish solar patterns such as the triskel and the spiral. Only a few examples of Class 1 solar double discs (but some Class 2 double discs) depict solar influences, as on the Shandwick Stone in Easter Ross. In *The Early Christian Monuments of Scotland* by Allen and Anderson, there are 16 examples of double discs triskel patterns on Pictish-Christian cross-slabs, which clearly show solar symbolism. Françoise Henry comments in the reproduction of *The Book of Kells* that the spiral patterns originally came from the solar helix. Romilly Allen compares the spirals on Iron Age metalwork and illuminated manuscripts, commenting that: 'These designs may have had a symbolic origin, as the triskel was a well-known sun symbol of the Bronze Age' (Allen 1904: 155).

These triskel symbols were very popular during the Iron Age and can be traced back – through metal work – to the double triple spirals carved into the kerbstone in front of the midwinter-aligned passage cairn of Newgrange. From this, it is easy to see how the powerful triple spirals of the sun were adopted into Irish Christianity and it is noteworthy that the symbols are also found at the centre of some Christian crosses in Ireland. Double discs with triskel spirals can also be seen on a number of pieces of Pictish silver, such as the Norrie's Law plaques and the ring terminal of the silver chain from Whitecleugh in Lanarkshire. Examples of solar triskels on Pictish double discs and at the centre of Crosses can be seen in Meigle Museum in Perthshire, while others are found in different part of the country. When the base of the Hilton Stone was excavated in its original position in 2000 at the west end of the Hilton Chapel, Dougie found that it was aligned to true north-south. The north triskel on the double disc turns clockwise, while the other turns in the other direction, and they could symbolise summer and winter. There is also a Gaelic tradition that positive rituals were carried out *desail*, in a clockwise direction with the sun. This can also be seen on the double discs on the Aberlemno roadside cross-slab.

Apparently, the early Christian Picts avoided depicting the figure of Christ at the crucifixion and chose instead to use their own powerful symbol.

THE EAST SIDE OF THE DINGWALL CUP MARKED PICTISH SYMBOL STONE NH 54930 58930
LAT. 57° 35' 49" N LONG. 4° 25' 44" W

Just inside the gates of St Clements's Church next to Tesco's in Dingwall, there is an early Pictish symbol stone that was found in the church in 1880 being used as the a doorway lintel. On the stone's east side near its top, there are three circles, two of which are joined to form a Double-Disc symbol. Below these there are six cup marks and a Crescent and V-Rod. The cup marks would suggest that it was a re-used Bronze Age stone.

THE WEST SIDE OF THE DINGWALL PICTISH SYMBOL STONE

The western side of the stone is carved with a Double-Disc and Z- Rod placed above some cup marks and two Crescent and V- Rods. Dingwall is named after the ancient Norse Thing (Tingvall) mound, in which the Earl of Cromarty was buried in 1714, and this was later marked by the obelisk seen in the background.

The Aberlemno Churchyard stone is one such slab, where a single disc containing triskels is placed at the centre of the cross. Such a position strongly suggests the cultural importance of the symbol, representing the centre of the Christian faith, for a common theme is that Christ is the light of the world. When Constantine made Christianity the first religion of the Roman Empire, the two main rivals had been the solar cults of Mithras and the Sol Invictus, Unconquered Sun, the symbolism of which the church adopted as the halo around Christ's head and rays of light emanating from the centre of the cross. As there were still beliefs in solar gods throughout Europe, it seems that the figure of Christ was introduced as the new incarnation of the sun god of everlasting life, tapping into deeply rooted traditions in order to convert people to the new belief. This would also explain why St Patrick in his Confession compares 'the worship of the sun which rises by the command of God, to the worship of the true sun which is Christ, the first leading to pain and damnation, the other to eternal life' (Mac Cana 1970: 32). Similar themes can be seen in the reference by Patrick the Bishop of the Hebrides, which states that, 'a church should be built wherever upright stones were found'. And, in Bede's *Ecclesiastical History of the English People*, in a letter to Abbot Mellitus from Pope Gregory, it is said that 'the pagan temples should not be destroyed but sanctified and made into churches'. The Irish Christians apparently understood that the simple double discs represented the sun and used this dual sacred symbolism on the cross-slabs to pull the two cultures together under the one faith. In time, as the political and religious doctrines within the Roman church changed, the solar symbolism was abandoned. The symbol of the sun on the Pictish cross-slabs was perhaps the last flicker of a belief that had lasted for over 4,000 years.

This book was initially inspired by the possible solar and lunar symbolism between Bronze Age cup marks and the Pictish double disc on the Clach Biorach at Edderton. It is suggested that this symbol, while still acting as a powerful ancestral tribal emblem, depicts the sun six months apart with the two crescents and represents the first and last phase of the moon during the lunar month. The Z-rod that cuts through the centre of the symbol is similar to that used on modern star maps for the sun's path through the sky over the course of the year and is called the ecliptic. The point where the Z-rod crosses the centre of the double disc could represent the position of the equinoxes. The Picts were still using an understanding of the solar-based representation of time that they had inherited from their ancestors.

Aberlemno, Angus

Standing next to the road in the village of Aberlemno, there are three Pictish symbol stones, comprising two Class 1 and a Class 2 Christian cross-slab. At the western end of the local churchyard, there is another magnificent Christian cross-slab. A photograph taken by Ritchie in 1906, which is held by the HES, shows the two Class 1 stones standing in the field on the other side of the wall. It is therefore very likely that these stones are still in their original positions, and that the wall was extended around them to make them accessible from the road. Other early Pictish symbol stones have been found nearby.

The two Class 1 Pictish stones are about 20 metres apart and are aligned north-east-south-west towards each other. The north-east stone is called the 'Serpent Stone', as it has on its western side a snake above a large double disc and Z-rod, a mirror, and comb. On the stone's other side, there are six large Bronze Age cup marks. The other Class 1 stone is called the 'Crescent Stone', from the faint crescent symbols on its western side. The chisel marks show

PICTISH CROSS SLAB, ABERLEMNO, ANGUS
NO 523 559 LAT. 56° 41' N. LONG. 2° 46' W

THE THREE PICTISH SYMBOL STONES TO THE SOUTH-WEST
NO 52276 55918 LAT. 56° 41' 33" N LONG. 2° 46' 51" W

From the 'Serpent Stone', the midwinter sun would have set in line with the Crescent Stone' some 3,000 years ago.

that this side of the stone had been refaced for these carvings, and the black lower half suggests that a fire was lit around its base. There are a number of cup marks on its narrow north-west edge. The fact that both of these stones are cup marked suggests that they are the remains of a Bronze Age alignment re-used by the Picts sometime between the 3rd and 6th centuries AD. Three thousand years ago, from the north-east cup marked stone, the sun would have set behind the south-west stone at midwinter. In the opposite direction, the north-east 'Pictish' stone would have pointed to where the northern full moon would have risen near the major standstill. As these stones do not appear to have been shifted and are bearing Bronze Age and Pictish symbols, does this mean that they were used over a 2,000-year period? For example, at midnight on 28 August 311 AD, a crescent moon in its last phase rose above the north-east stone. Although this would have occurred many times since the stones were erected, does this explain the crescent symbol on the stone's western side?

To the top of the stone are a large Crescent and V-rod, a solar double disc and a Z-rod. Below these is a hunting scene with horsemen, trumpeters, a centaur and Daniel killing a lion. These images are similar to those on the Nigg and Shandwick Stones, so perhaps they were carved by the same sculptor.

ABERLEMNO CHURCHYARD PICTISH CROSS SLAB
NO 52239 55554 LAT. 56° 41' 21" N LONG. 2° 46' 53" W

The Picts did not carve the crucifixion on their cross-slabs, and as shown on the Aberlemno church Cross-Slab in Angus, they used a Sun Disc to symbolise Christ as the life giving sun when he said, 'for I am the light of the world'.

BOXED-IN ABERLEMNO ROADSIDE PICTISH STONES

The three stones are boxed to protect them from frost during the winter. Although the wall made it difficult to photograph, the midwinter sun set behind the boxed-in south-west symbol stone at 3:00pm on 10 December 2001. During the Bronze Age the sun would have set nearer the base of the stone. As other Pictish symbol stones have been found around Aberlemno, the Christians probably set up their stones there as it was already a centre of Pictish political power.

Conclusion

In this work we have attempted to give an overview of thousands of years of Scotland's past through the consideration of ancient monuments. It is manifestly clear that there are factors which retain a fundamental importance in the raising of these monuments over millennia. Most obviously, as Dougie's surveys show, are the solar and lunar alignments. Whether we think our ancestors saw the sun as a form of godhead or something more practical matters little. What matters is that the evidence is irrefutable and the continuing use of alignments in funerary monuments suggest so much more than a calendric awareness of the passage of both sun and moon. This is not to diminish the importance of the calendar to the pastoral peoples of this part of the world. The centrality in both oral tradition and ritual practice of the agriculturally important cross-quarter days of Imbolc, Beltane, Lughnasad and Samhain is such that they can be seen as being as important in how people marked the passage of the year as the equinoxes and solstices.

It is in the process of such dates, which are essentially human-created, becoming so significant, that we can see something else. The fact that the alignments occur in so many monuments that have a funerary aspect is patently obvious and it is reverence for the dead, those who went before, the ancestors, that creates the very concept of funerary monument.

In paying attention to the folklore of so many monuments, time and again we meet the same ideas. While some sites and natural locations are directly linked to clearly supernatural creatures, spirits or even godhead figures, the underlying concept we are faced with is that of the ancestors, something we share with human societies through space and time.

We can see that the Sidhe are the spirit ancestors in their sitheans or burial mounds that dot the landscape, and in others they are presented as the Picts, though in the oral tradition these beings are not bound by the hoped-for precision of historical reference.

While the focus of this book has been on the interpretation of physical evidence and related folklore up to the Pictish period, the ancestors lived on. Reverence for them remained part of the tribal structures that lived on in Highland society till the eighteenth century and the evidence suggests probably in the Borders till a couple of centuries earlier. The very use of the clan names was reference back to the idea of a common ancestry and today's ever-growing interest in Scottish genealogy shows how deep-rooted such ideas remain.

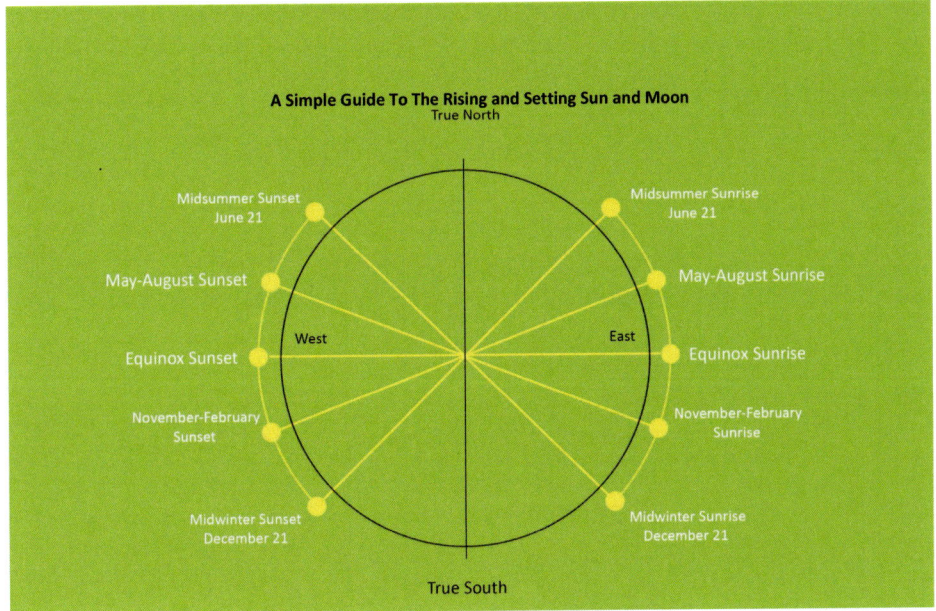

A Simple Guide to the Rising and Setting Sun and Moon

The archaeoastronomy surveys can be difficult to understand, so these have been simplified to the times when the sun or moon will rise or set in line with the monuments. The illustration shows from a central 'you are here' position how the sun rises and sets along the circle of the horizon at eight divisions of the year, from midwinter to midsummer and back again. Each of the divisions occurs about every 45 days, ie 8 x 45 = 360 days. These times are midsummer and midwinter (21 June and December), the Equinoxes (21 March and September) and the summer and winter cross quarter times in early May and August and early November and February. To align a monument to, say, the midsummer sunrise would only require watching the sun until it rose in the same position over a few days and marking it with two aligned sticks in the ground. The monument would then be built around this alignment.

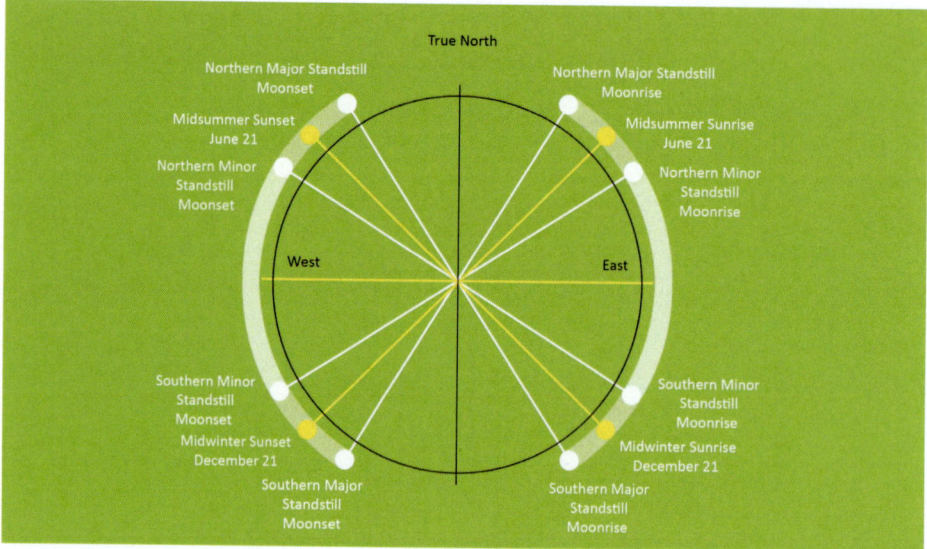

The moon also has northern and southern extremes and, because it circles the earth every month, it rises and sets along the horizon between these extremes every 28 days. The time when the extreme northern and southern moon rises and sets beyond the sun's midsummer and midwinter positions is called the major standstill. Although the lunar cycle is 18.61 years, as the moon can reach these northern and southern extremes every month for about a year, this can occur for about 20 years. After about a year, the moon's northern and southern extremes start to contract slightly every month and, after about ten years, it reaches its minor standstill positions, where the moon will rise and set within the positions of the midsummer and midwinter sun. After about a year, the moon's northern and southern rising and setting positions start to expand along the horizon for about ten years until it again reaches its major standstill positions. This pattern then repeats itself. Although the monuments were only generally aligned to the sun at the eight divisions of the year, and for the moon near its northern and southern extremes, it is likely that our prehistoric ancestors had a fairly accurate solar/lunar calendar.

References

Allen, R, *Celtic Art in Pagan and Christian Times*, London, 1904.
Anderson, J, *A Tour Through the Islands of Orkney and Schetland*, Oxford, 1879.
Ashmore, P, 'Neolithic carvings in Maes Howe [related to Skara Brae etc]' in *Proceedings of the Society of Antiquaries of Scotland*, 1987.
Bain, G, *The Stone Circles at Clava*, Transactions of the Gaelic Society of Inverness, Inverness, 1886.
Ballachulish (Accessed: www.sath.org.uk/edscot/www.educationscotland.gov.uk/scotlandshistory/earlypeople/ballachulishgoddesb/index.html).
Barclay, G & Maxwell, GS, 'Cleaven Dyke (Caputh and Lethendy) parishes, cursus monument/bank barrow' from *Discovery and excavation in Scotland*, Edinburgh, 1995.
—'Excavations on the Cleaven Dyke and Littleour, south-east Perthsire, Past' from *Newsletter of the Prehistoric Society*, London, 1996.
—*The Cleaven Dyke and Littleour: Monuments in the Neolithic of Tayside*, Edinburgh, 1998.
—'Metropolitan' and 'Parochial'/'Core' and 'Periphery': a Historiography of the Neolithic of Scotland' in *Proceedings of the Prehistoric Society*, Cambridge, 2001.
Bede, *A History of the English Church and People* (trans. Sherley-Price, L), London, 1968.
Bradley, R & Sheridan, A, 'Croftmoraig and the Chronology of Stone Circles' in *Proceedings of the Prehistoric Society*, Cambridge, 2014.
Bradley, R & Watson, A, *Ben Lawers: carved rocks on a loud mountain* in *Visualising the Neolithic* (eds. Cochrane, A & Jones, AM), Oxford, 2012.
Bradley, R, 'The Good Stones, a new investigation of the Clava Cairns' in *Society of Antiquaries of Scotland*, Edinburgh, 2000.
Bradley, R. & Nimura, C, *The Use and Re-use of Stone Circles*, Oxford, 2016.
Broun, D, 'The genealogical 'tractates' associated with Míniugud senchusa fher nAlban and the creation of the Dál Riata ancestry of kings of Alba' in *Northern Scotland*, 2006.
Burl, A, 'By the light of the cinerary moon' from *Astronomy and Society in Britain During the Period 4000–1500 BC* (eds. Ruggles, CLN & Whittle, AWR), Oxford, 1981.
—*A Guide to the Stone Circles of Britain, Ireland and Brittany*, New Haven, 2005.
—*The Stone circles of the British Isles*, New Haven, 1979.
Burt, E, *Burt's Letters from the North of Scotland*, Edinburgh, 1998.
Caesar (Accessed: thelatinreadingblog.blogspot.com/2013/07/caesar-de-bello-gallico-613-14-about.html).
Campbell, E, 'Were the Scots Irish?' from *Antiquity*, Cambridge, 2015.
Campbell, M & Sandeman, MLS, 'Mid Argyll: a field survey of the historic and prehistoric monuments' from *Proceedings of the Society of Antiquaries of Scotland*, 1962.
CANMORE (Accessed: canmore.org.uk).
Coles, FR, 'Notice of Standing Stones, Cists, and hitherto unrecorded Cup-and-Ring-marks in various localities' from *Proceedings of the Society of Antiquaries of Scotland*, 1905.
Coles, FR, 'Report on Stone Circles in Perthshire, principally Strathearn, with measured Plans and Drawings (obtained under the Gunning Fellowship)' from *Proceedings of the Society of Antiquaries of Scotland*, 1910.
Cowie, T, 'Excavations at Kintraw, Argyll, 1979' from *Glasgow Archaeological Journal*, 1980.
Craw, J, 'Excavations at Dunadd and at other Sites on the Poltalloch Estates, Argyll' from *Proceedings of the Society of Antiquaries of Scotland*, 1930.
Curle, A, 'Fourth Report and Inventory of Monuments and Constructions in Galloway' from Royal Commission on the Ancient and Historical Monuments of Scotland, 1912.
Davidson, HRE, *Gods and Myths of Northern Europe*, London, 1960.
DES, *Discovery and Excavation Scotland* (https://archaeologydataservice.ac.uk/archives).
Evans-Wentz, WY, *The Fairy-Faith in Celtic Countries*, London, 2009.

Farrer, J, 'Maes Howe. Notice of runic inscriptions discovered during recent excavations in the Orkneys', 1862 (Accessed: archive.org).
Feast (Accessed: news.nationalgeographic.com/news/2012/120127-stonehenge-ness-brodgar-scotland-science/).
Frazer, JG, *The Golden Bough*, London, 1890.
Freuchen, P, *Book of the Eskimos*, London, 1961.
Gabala (Accessed: sejh.pagesperso-orange.fr/keltia/leborgab/dedannan-r1.html).
Gantz, J, *Early Irish Myths and Sagas*, London, 2000.
Genetics (Accessed: www.eurekalert.org.pub_releases/2017-02/uu-gds022117.php).
Gimbutas, M, *The Civilization of the Goddess: The World of Old Europe*, London, 1994.
Gobekli Tepe (Accessed: www.smithsonianmag.com/history/gobekli-tepe-the-worlds-first-temple-83613665/).
Gregorson Campbell, J, *The Gaelic Otherworld: Superstitions of the Highlands and the Islands and Witchcraft and Second Sight in the Highlands and Islands of Scotland* (ed. Black, R), Edinburgh, 2005.
Harmon, M, *The Colloquy of the Old Man*, Washington DC, 2002.
Hawkins, G, 'Discovery and Excavation in Scotland' from *Archaeology Scotland*, 2007.
—*Mindsteps to the Cosmos*, Singapore, 2002.
Herodotus (Accessed: classics.mit.edu/Herodotus/history.4.iv.html).
Isaacs, J, *Australian Dreaming: 40,000 years of Aboriginal History*, London, 1979.
Joass, JM, 'Note of Five Kists found under a Tumulus on the Glebe of the Parish of Eddertoun, Ross, and of a Kist within a Circle of Standing Stones in the same Neighbourhood' from *The Society of Antiquaries of Scotland*, 1866.
Jones, A, *An Animate Landscape: Rock Art and the Prehistory of Kilmartin, Argyll, Scotland*, Oxford, 2011.
Kinnes, I, 'Astronomy and Society in Britain during the period 4000–1500 BC' from *Archaeological Journal* (eds. Ruggles, C & Whittle, AWR), Oxford, 1982.
Kirk, R, *The Secret Commonwealth of Elves, Fauns and Fairies*, New York, 2008.
LaViolette, P & McIntosh, A, 'Fairy hills: merging heritage and conservation' from *Ecos – A Review of Conservation*, 1997.
Lebor Gabala (Accessed: sejh.pagersperso-orange.fr/keltia/leborgab/dedannan-r1.html).
Lewis, D, *The Voyaging Stars: Secrets of the Pacific Island Navigators*, London, 1979.
Mac Cana, P, *Celtic Mythology*, London, 1973.
Mackenzie, JB, 'Notes of some Cup-marked Stones and Rocks near Kenmore, and their Folk-Lore' from *The Society of Antiquaries of Scotland*, 1899.
MacKie, EW *The Megalith Builders*, London, 1977.
 —'Maeshowe and the winter solstice: ceremonial aspects of the Orkney Grooved Ware culture' from *Antiquity* 71: 338-59, 1997.
Macpherson, GW, *Highland Myths and Legends*, Edinburgh, 2001.
Martin, M, *A Description of the Western Isles*, Edinburgh, 1976.
Marwick, EW, *The Folklore of Orkney and Shetland*, Edinburgh, 2011.
McHardy, SA, *A New History of the Picts*, Edinburgh, 2010.
 —*Pagan Symbols of the Picts*, Edinburgh, 2012.
 —*Scotland: Myth, Legend and Folklore*, Edinburgh, 2000.
 —*Scotland's Future Culture*, Edinburgh, 2017.
 —*The Quest for the Nine Maidens*, Edinburgh, 2003.
McNeill, M, *The Silver Bough: Scottish Folklore and Folk-belief*, Edinburgh, 2001.
Migration (Accessed: www.biorxiv.org/content/early/2015/02/10/013433).
Morris, R & Thomson, B, 'Torbhlaren, Kilmichael-Glassary,Cup-marked rock' from *Discovery and excavation in Scotland*, Edinburgh, 1969.
Morris, RWB, 'The cup-and-ring marks and similar sculptures of Scotland: a survey of the southern counties, Part II' from *The Society of Antiquaries of Scotland*, 1968.
Mythogram 1 (Accessed: www.youtube.com/watch?v=Ls1HGq3XkF4).
NLS (Accessed: maps.nls.uk/geo/explore/#/).

O'Kelly, MJ, *Newgrange: Archaeology, Art and Legend*, London, 1988.
Patrick (Accessed: catholicplanet.com/ebooks/Confession-of-St-Patrick.pdf).
Peltenburg, EJ, *Excavation of Culcharron Cairn, Benderlock, Argyll* from *The Society of Antiquaries of Scotland*, 1972.
Piggott, S & Simpson, DDA, 'Excavation of a Stone Circle at Croft Moraig, Perthshire, Scotland' from *Proceedings of the Prehistoric Society*, 2014.
Ponting, G & M, *The Standing Stones of Calanais*, 1977.
Richards, C, 'Monuments as Landscape: Creating the Centre of the World in Late Neolithic Orkney' from *World Archaeology*, 1996.
Richards, C, 'Survey and Excavation of Barnhouse, Stenness, Orkney' (Unpublished report, University of Glasgow).
  —*Building the Great Stone Circles of the North*, Oxford, 2013.
Richardson, D, *Laggan, Past and Present*, Laggan, 1990.
Ritchie, J & Marwick, EW, *The Stones of Stenness, Orkney* from *The Society of Antiquaries of Scotland*, 1976.
Ritchie, J, 'Notes on some Aberdeenshire Sculptured Stones and Crosses' from *The Society of Antiquaries of Scotland*, 1914.
Rivet, ALF & Smith, C, *The Place Names of Roman Britain*, London, 1979.
Ross, A, *Folklore of the Scottish Highlands*, London, 1990.
Ruggles, CLN & Burl, HAW, 'A New Study of the Aberdeenshire Recumbent Stone Circles, 2: Interpretation' from *Journal for the History of Astronomy, Archaeoastronomy Supplement, Cambridge*, 1985.
Scott, D, 'An Astronomical Assessment of Three Groups of Standing Stones in Strath Spey, Scotland' from *The Journal of Archaeoastronomy*, Austin, 1990.
  —'Recent Astronomical observations at Kilmartin Glen, Argyll, Scotland' (Accessed: www.antiquity.ac.uk/projgall/scott324/).
  —'The Solar Lunar Orientations of the Orkney-Cromarty and Clava Cairns' from *Journal of Skyscape Archaeology*, 2016.
  —*An Astronomical Assessment of the Clava Cairns*. Copy held by the author and HES, Edinburgh, 1992.
  —*The Clava Cairns*, Tain, 2010.
  —*The Stones of the Pictish Peninsulas*, 2004.
Scott, JG, 'The Stone Circles at Temple Wood, Kilmartin, Argyll' from *Scottish Archaeological Journal*, 1988.
Sheridan, JA, 'The National Museums Scotland radiocarbon dating programmes: results obtained during 2004/5' from *Discovery and Excavation in Scotland*, 2005.
Simpson, DDA, 'Excavations at Kintraw, Argyll' from *The Society of Antiquaries of Scotland*, 1968.
Spence, M, *Standing Stones and Maeshowe of Stenness*, Spean Bridge, 1946.
Stewart, MEC, 'The excavation of standing stones at Lundin Farm, near Aberfeldy, Perthshire' from *The Society of Antiquaries of Scotland*, 1965.
Swire, O, *Outer Hebrides and Their Legends*, Edinburgh, 1966.
Symson, A, 'A Large Description of Galloway' from *Geographical Collections Relating to Scotland* (ed. Macfarlane, W), Edinburgh, 1906.
Tehrani, J, www.dur.ac.uk/news/research/?itemno=27041, 2016.
Thom, A, *Megalithic Lunar Observatories*, Oxford, 1970.
  —*Megalithic Sites in Britain*, Oxford, 1967.
  —www.soue.org.uk/souenews/issue8/thom.html, 2009.
Thomas, C, 'The Interpretation of the Pictish Symbols' from *Archaeological Journal*, 2014.
  —*And Shall These Mute Stones Speak? Post-Roman Inscriptions in Western Britain*, Cardiff, 1994.
Watson, WJW, *The Celtic Place-Names of Scotland*, Edinburgh, 2004.
Welfare, S & Fairley, J, Arthur C. Clarke's Mysterious World. London, 1980.
Wifie (Accessed: www.orkneyjar.com/archaeology/linksofnoltland/venus.htm).
Young, A & Mitchell, MEC, *'Report on excavation at Monzie'* from *The Society of Antiquaries of Scotland*, 1938.

Luath Press Limited

committed to publishing well written books worth reading

LUATH PRESS takes its name from Robert Burns, whose little collie Luath (*Gael.*, swift or nimble) tripped up Jean Armour at a wedding and gave him the chance to speak to the woman who was to be his wife and the abiding love of his life. Burns called one of the 'Twa Dogs' Luath after Cuchullin's hunting dog in Ossian's *Fingal*. Luath Press was established in 1981 in the heart of Burns country, and is now based a few steps up the road from Burns' first lodgings on Edinburgh's Royal Mile. Luath offers you distinctive writing with a hint of unexpected pleasures.

Most bookshops in the UK, the US, Canada, Australia, New Zealand and parts of Europe, either carry our books in stock or can order them for you. To order direct from us, please send a £sterling cheque, postal order, international money order or your credit card details (number, address of cardholder and expiry date) to us at the address below. Please add post and packing as follows: UK – £1.00 per delivery address; overseas surface mail – £2.50 per delivery address; overseas airmail – £3.50 for the first book to each delivery address, plus £1.00 for each additional book by airmail to the same address. If your order is a gift, we will happily enclose your card or message at no extra charge.

Luath Press Limited
543/2 Castlehill
The Royal Mile
Edinburgh EH1 2ND
Scotland
Telephone: +44 (0)131 225 4326 (24 hours)
email: sales@luath.co.uk
Website: www.luath.co.uk